New American Cuisine
for Today's Family

New American Cuisine for Today's Family

Fresh Ideas to Prepare Healthy Mediterranean Meals in Under 30 Minutes

Lisa Akoury-Ross

SWEET DREAMS PUBLISHING
of Massachusetts

SWEET DREAMS PUBLISHING
of Massachusetts

New American Cuisine for Today's Family
Cover & Interior Design: Lisa Akoury-Ross
Published by Sweet Dreams Publishing of Massachusetts
5 Federal Street
Weymouth, MA 02188

For more information about this book contact Lisa Akoury-Ross at Sweet Dreams Publishing by email at
lross@publishatsweetdreams.com

To obtain permission(s) to use material from this work, please submit a written request to
Sweet Dreams Publishing of MA,
Permissions Department
5 Federal Street Weymouth, MA 02188

or email your request to info@publishatsweetdreams.com

Library of Congress Control Number: 2009928680

ISBN-10: 0-9824461-1-X
ISBN-13: 978-0-9824461-1-9

Printed in the United States of America

Photo credits:
Cover & title page: All photos courtesy of Morguefile.com
Pages 26, 36, 64, 75, 84, 94: IStockphoto.com
Marginal photos: family dinner: IStockphoto.com; kids with balloons: Fotosearch.com

Dedication

For my husband Ron, our children Ben and Halle
and our sweet dog, Blizzard.
You make me a better wife and mother each day.

For my late cousin, Lenny. I live in the moment because of you.

Me and my sisters from left to right/top to bottom: Michele, me, Jennifer, and Jackie.

I was born in an Italian and Lebanese family with three sisters. We grew up in a home where good food and large family gatherings were the norm. As a child, there was always someone cooking for us—grandparents, aunts, and uncles—in addition to our own parents—so there was always something good to eat in my house. My friends also enjoyed coming over and seeing what was in our kitchen. In the town I grew up in, Braintree, Massachusetts, the families that settled there were predominately Irish. There were only a few Lebanese families, let alone the combination of Italian and Lebanese, so my friends still reflect on how interesting it was to join my family for dinner.

Today a lot of these Mediterranean meals have become a part of American cuisine. Many fine restaurants are adding exotic spices and European flavors to their menus, therefore coining the name "New American Cuisine." Hummus, tabouli and pita bread used to be unfamiliar foods to many Americans, but now they are a large part of many American diets. And since it has been reported in many medical journals and other publications that the Mediterranean diet is responsible for longer and healthier lives, people are turning to traditional Mediterranean dishes for healthy options to bring to their dinner tables[1,2].

Now that my grandparents have passed away, and my parents, aunts and uncles are all getting older and cooking less, I realized that it's time to pick their brains and carry on the family tradition of fine Mediterranean cuisine—only I needed to figure out a way to prepare these dishes in a short amount of time.

[1] http://www.sciencedaily.com/releases/2009/01/090122081334.htm
[2] http://www.medicinalfoodnews.com/vol02/issue2/longlife

Over the past 10 years, as a working mother of two, I have learned that in order to offer my family the good food that I grew up with, I needed to be creative and cut corners to accommodate our busy schedule. Another challenge in trying to duplicate this healthy lifestyle was to cut down on my grocery bill and find ways to make purchases less often. I remember my mother and aunt used to go to the grocery store almost daily to pick up things for that evening's dinner or for the next day! Together with my three sisters, and the help of my parents, Aunt and Uncle, I have discovered clever ways to serve great meals during the week that will not cost a small fortune or keep me away from my home more than I already am.

My final challenge was to prepare one meal for the entire family. After a couple of years getting bamboozled into making two or three different meals for my family each night, I realized this had to stop. My husband and I were also up to our eyeballs in serving Mac 'n Cheese, pizza, and plain pasta each night for dinner. Most parents of small children would agree that it's a struggle to find several healthy meals that the whole family can enjoy.

For those of you working parents who are the primary cooks in the house, with very little time and a tight budget, this book is for you! You will find ideas to make quick full-course meals for an average family of 4-6 people. It is guaranteed to get healthy and nutritious meals on the table in less than 30 minutes for very little money. You will find the itemized lists in these menus are mostly things that you already have in your pantry, refrigerator or freezer, making meal-time much easier!

I hope you enjoy trying out these recipes as much as I have!

—Lisa Akoury-Ross

My husband, Ron and our children, Ben and Halle

 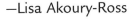

✧ Contents ✧

✧Beginnings 11
  Simple salad for 4 11
  Simple salad dressing. 12
  Other salad ideas. 13
  Variations to Simple salad dressing 15
  Marinated four-bean salad. 17
  Sito's Fatoosh 18
  Gido's Tabouli 18
  Feta & calamata olive dip 20
  Mediterranean fruit & cheese tarts 20
  Roasted eggplant tahini (Baba ghanoush). 21
  Spinach & pine nut triangles 22
  Pita & gorgonzola nachos 23
  Tangy yogurt spread. 23
  Zesty lemon hummus 24
  Quick homemade salsa 24
  Bill's salsa 25

✧Crock Pot Meals 27
  Anna's minestrone soup 28
  Mluhea in a crock pot (Mediterranean chicken & garlic stew) 29
  Nonnie's pasta fazool 31
  Chicken & spinach stew 32
  Aunt Lee's marinara sauce 33
  Piccata in a crock pot 34
  Lemony lentil soup 35

✧Family Favorites 37
  Basic sauté 37
  Sautéed chicken, mushroom and artichoke hearts 38
  Seafood sauté—spanish style 40
  10-minute fra diavlo. 41
  Linguini & clam sauce. 42
  Tandoori chicken 43
  Your pantry's house stew 44
  White chili 45
  Escarole and beans with sausage. 47
  Veggie burgers (Falafel) 48
  Mediterranean gumbo. 50
  Meat Pies (Fatayer) 51
  Spinach pies (Spinach fatayer) 52
  Mediterranean meatloaf (Kibbie) 53
  Lebanese barbecue chicken (Shish tawook) 54
  Lentils & rice 55

✧ Contents ✧

Blackened tuscan swordfish. 56
Marinated salmon steaks 57
Marinated chicken breasts. 57
Pasta primavera 58
Grape leaves 59
Uncle Rudy's pasta bolognese 61
Flavorful meatballs 63

✧Summer Delights **65**
Lisa's lazy summer lemonade 65
Iced mint tea 66
Quick gazpacho 67
Uncle John's grilled lemon & garlic chicken 68
Grilled marinated swordfish. 69
Shish kebab 70
Marinated steak tips 71
Minty potato salad 72
Mediterranean grilled vegetables 73

✧Quick & Healthy Side Dishes **75**
Mediterranean rice 75
Spanish rice 76
Indian rice 77
Half-the-time fresh baked potatoes 78
Candied sweet potatoes 78
5-minute lemon broccoli 79
5-minute cooked spinach 79
5-minute bean medley 80
Sauteed green beans & tomato (Luby) 81
Sauteéd chickpeas 82
Ratatouille 83

✧Guiltless Desserts **85**
Lower fat baklava. 85
Greek shortbread cookies 87
Rice pudding 89
Italian anise cookies. 90
Anise biscotti 91
low-fat, low-cholesterol chocolate chip cookies 92
low-fat, low-cholesterol congo bars 93

✧Planning Ahead **95**

✧About the Author **99**

In the past, I found it surprising that whenever I tossed together my basic salad, people actually raved over it. I later realized that others were not accustomed to such variety in an every day salad. But on the kids' "PB&J" or "Mac 'n Cheese Nights", I often make a complete meal for myself and my husband that starts with my simple salad, adding whatever vegetables, meats or cheeses I have in the house. Your salad doesn't have to be boring; be creative!

Simple Salad for 4

1 package of lettuce (Boston Bib, Romaine or Mediterranean Mix)

½ cup diced or halved ripe tomatoes (on the vine, cherry or campello)

½ cup English cucumber, diced and peeled

¼ cup diced red onion or diced scallions including some of the green

½ of a 10-oz can chickpeas, drained

¼ cup loosely packed fresh flat-leaf parsley

Combine all ingredients in one bowl large enough to toss. Toss with Simple Salad Dressing (see next page for recipe) or other creative salad dressings from page 15.

Other ideas for your salad:

Add or substitute ingredients like hearts of palm, artichoke hearts, calamata olives, cooked pasta, beans of any kind, and meats, including cold cuts.

Instead of a combination of herbs use all mint, all parsley, or all basil to add different flavors each time you make a salad for your family.

Ideas for your picky eater:

As picky as my kids are when it comes to dinner, they enjoy my simple salad! They love the salad dressing, eat only the cucumbers and tomatoes, and avoid the rest.

Simple Salad Dressing

As simple as this dressing is, I get more compliments from this simple salad and dressing from a variety of people with different tastes. The trick is finding the right portion of each ingredient to suit your taste!

Sweet balsamic vinegar

Extra virgin olive oil

Sea salt & fresh ground pepper to taste

2 pinches of garlic powder

Once your salad is prepared, slowly drizzle with balsamic vinegar, using just a small amount at a time. Lightly toss, and then drizzle with extra virgin olive oil. Add remaining ingredients, then add the sea salt and pepper to taste. Continue to add, toss and taste ingredients until you reach your desired flavor. Top with fresh chopped parsley.

Other Salad Ideas

Try these varying salad recipes to find your family's favorite. Toss with Simple Salad Dressing, or any of the other choices found on page 15.

Mediterranean Salad

Simple Salad (see page 11)

2 tbsp fresh mint, chopped

1 14.5 oz can quartered artichoke hearts

½ cup pitted calamata olives

Crumbled feta or goat cheese

Serve with toasted pita bread drizzled with olive oil and sprinkled with sea salt

Broccoli Lover's Salad

Simple Salad (see page 11)

1 cup frozen broccoli florettes (cooking instructions below)

2 tbsp olive oil

2 tbsp lemon juice

Sea salt (to taste)

Place broccoli in microwaveable dish. Drizzle with olive oil and lemon juice and sprinkle with sea salt. Cover with an airtight lid and microwave on High for 3½ minutes. If using frozen broccoli with stems, cook for an additional 1½ minutes. Carefully remove dish from microwave and let stand uncovered for a few minutes until it cools off.

This cooked broccoli makes a great side dish with any meal!

Southwestern Salad

Simple Salad (see page 11)

1 cup tortilla chips, slightly crushed

1 cup of your favorite salsa (I like southwestern salsa with corn & beans)

Line your salad bowl with the crushed tortilla chips. Add the simple salad and toss lightly, using the salsa as your dressing.

Dried Cranberry and Almonds

Simple Salad (see page 11)

¼ cup dried cranberries

⅛ cup sliced almonds (plain or honey roasted)

Simple Salad Dressing (see page 12)

Toss all ingredients together in large salad bowl and serve.

Simple Salad Antipasto Style

Simple Salad (see page 11 and substitute mint for 2 tbsp chopped fresh basil)

Pitted Calamata olives

Sliced Italian cold cuts (i.e.: prosciutto, salami, and/or mortadella)

Italian cheese(s) (provolone, mozzarella, etc.) chopped into bite sized blocks

Pepperoncinis (to taste)

Simple Salad Dressing (see page 12)

Toss all ingredients together in large salad bowl and serve.

Variations to Simple Salad Dressing

Balsamic & Mustard Vinaigrette Dressing

½ cup extra virgin olive oil

½ cup sweet balsamic vinegar

1 tsp Dijon mustard

1 small clove of fresh garlic, minced (or ½ tsp garlic powder)

½ tsp sea salt (or to taste)

freshly ground pepper to taste

1 tbsp each fresh chopped basil and parsley (or ½ tsp each dried)

Combine all ingredients and wisk well. Place in a container with a tight lid. Will keep at room temperature for up to two weeks. You can also store this in the refrigerator, but the oil will solidify, so keep it at room temperature about 10 minutes before use.

Non-Fat Vinaigrette & Mustard Salad Dressing

½ cup sweet balsamic vinegar

½ cup water

1 tsp Dijon mustard

1 small clove of fresh garlic, minced (or ½ tsp garlic powder)

½ tsp sea salt (or to taste)

freshly ground pepper to taste

1 tbsp each fresh chopped basil and parsley (or ½ tsp each dried)

Combine all ingredients and wisk well. Place in a container with a tight lid. Will store at room temperature for up to two weeks.

Southwestern Salad Dressing

¼ cup extra virgin olive oil

½ cup fresh or bottled lime juice

1 small clove garlic, minced

¼ cup fresh chopped cilantro

¼ tsp cumin

1 tsp sea salt

Fresh ground pepper (to taste)

Combine all ingredients in a container with a tight lid. Dressing can be stored in refrigerator for up to two weeks. Oil will solidify, so allow to stand at room temperature for about 10 minutes before serving.

Mediterranean Salad Dressing

¼ cup extra virgin olive oil

½ cup fresh or bottled lemon juice

1 small clove garlic, minced

½ cup fresh chopped mint

1 tsp sea salt

Fresh ground pepper (to taste)

Combine all ingredients in a container with a tight lid. Dressing can be stored in refrigerator for up to two weeks. Oil will solidify, so allow to stand at room temperature for about 10 minutes before serving.

Marinated Four Bean Salad

2 cups frozen cut green beans

2 cups frozen cut wax beans

1 cup match-stick sized raw carrots

1 small red onion, diced

1 15.5 oz can red kidney beans, rinsed and well drained

1 15.5 oz can chickpeas, well drained

1 15.5 oz can quartered artichoke hearts, well drained

¼ cup fresh chopped flat leaf parsley

1 tbsp fresh chopped basil

½ cup Simple Salad Dressing (see page 12 for recipe)

Blanch green beans, wax beans and carrots in boiling water for four minutes.

Drain and rinse with cold water. Place beans and carrots in large mixing bowl. Add ¼ cup of salad dressing and toss. Combine the remaining ingredients and pour in more dressing. Let marinate and chill for at least an hour. Adjust seasonings if necessary and serve over a bed of lettuce, a simple salad or by itself as a cold side dish.

Makes a great side dish for any summer cookout!

See page 65 for other summer menu ideas.

Sito's Fatoosh

1 large loaf Lebanese bread, or two small loaves pita bread, cut on the seam to make two round halves

1 bag lettuce of your choice

¼ cup diced scallions

½ cup cucumber, peeled and diced

¼ cup fresh chopped mint

½ cup chickpeas, drained

Toast bread until brown on both sides. Once cooled, break apart into bite sized pieces. Place in large mixing bowl. Add remaining ingredients. Pour Mediterranean Salad Dressing (see page 16 for recipe) and toss well. Serve immediately.

Gido's Tabouli

Tabouli isn't exactly a *quick* dish to prepare—there's a good amount of chopping involved. But I can honestly say it is well worth it!

2 bunches flat leaf parsley, washed well, and tough stems cut and discarded

¼ cup fresh chopped mint

1 cup quick absorbing cracked wheat (also known as bulgur wheat)* **

1½ cups cold drinking water

6 or 7 large vine ripened tomatoes, diced into small cubes (use very ripe, juicy tomatoes).

¼ cup extra virgin olive oil

Juice of 5 or 6 ripe lemons, or approx 1 cup bottled lemon juice

2–3 tsp sea salt (or to taste)

Continues

*You can find cracked wheat in the International or rice isle of most supermarkets. Fast absorbing cracked wheat can also be found in Mediterranean markets.

Place the cracked wheat in a medium-sized mixing bowl and cover with the water. Let sit uncovered in refrigerator for about 20 minutes, or until all the water is absorbed.

Prep the rest of the ingredients while wheat is resting: Finely chop the two bunches of parsley, including the tender part of the stems, and place in large mixing bowl. Add the diced tomatoes and fresh mint.

Check to see if wheat is ready by mixing to see if there is any extra water at the bottom of bowl. If there is, continue to mix and set aside for another 10 minutes or so. Once water is fully absorbed, add the wheat to the parsley and tomato mixture, and mix thoroughly. Add more tomatoes if desired. Drizzle the extra virgin olive oil and lemon juice slowly, adding just a bit at a time, along with the sea salt. Continue to mix and add more oil, lemon juice, and/or sea salt as necessary to suit your taste.

Note that the cracked wheat will absorb a good amount of the juice from the tomatoes and lemon juice; check the flavor 30 minutes after preparation to ensure no flavor was lost. You may choose to add more of the dressing.

Serve cold, with large romaine lettuce leaves or pita bread.

Other ideas for your salad:

Another great summer dish to go with any cookout menu! Fresh garden tomatoes & lemons make this an outstanding salad!

See page 65 for other summer menu ideas.

**I've been known to "cheat" and purchase a boxed package of tabouli in the prepared rice isle at the local grocery store. I use only the cracked wheat that comes separate from the spice pack. Discard the spice pack and follow the recipe above.

This also makes a great spread over French bread baked with olive oil and sea salt, or in plain, fresh pita loaves.

Feta & Calamata Olive Dip

This is a great quick appetizer that can be served immediately or prepared several days in advance.

1 small whole clove garlic

1 15½ oz can chickpeas with half of its juice

¼ cup extra virgin olive oil

¾ cup crumbled feta cheese

½ cup pitted calamata olives

5 sprigs fresh flat leaf Italian parsley

Combine all ingredients in blender or food processor. Blend for a few seconds then stir to be sure the thicker ingredients are blending in well with the rest. Continue to blend and stir until well processed.*

Serve chilled or room temperature with pita, crackers or tortilla chips

Mediterranean Fruit & Cheese Tarts

2- 2 oz packages mini filo dough shells

5 oz sharp cheese of your choice (Gorgonzola, Drunken Goat, or Extra Sharp Cheddar, etc.)

½ jar mango chutney

¼ cup slivered almonds

Preheat oven to 375 degrees. Place filo cups on a baking sheet. In each cup, add a block of cheese, almost filling the tart. Add ½ tsp mango chutney on top, and top again with a sprinkle of slivered almonds. Bake uncovered for about 15-20 minutes, or until cheese filling is bubbling and the filo dough is lightly browned.

* If you find the consistency too dry to process, try adding a few tablespoons of chickpea juice or olive oil.

Roasted Eggplant Tahini

(Baba Ghanoush)

1 large eggplant

2 cloves garlic, minced

2 tbsp tahini paste

⅛ cup fresh lemon juice (or bottled)

Sea salt (to taste)

1 dash hot sauce (or to taste)

4 sprigs fresh parsley

Olive oil

Preheat oven to 375 degrees. Trim the ends of the eggplant, slice down the middle lengthwise and place on baking sheet, skin side down. Bake for 15-20 minutes, or until well cooked through and skin is blackened. Remove from oven and allow to cool. Scoop out inside of eggplant with a large spoon and place in blender. Add garlic, tahini paste, lemon juice, salt, 2 sprigs of chopped parsley and hot sauce. Blend to smooth consistency.

Serve cold or at room temperature on a flat plate or shallow bowl. Drizzle with olive oil and garnish with 2 remaining sprigs of parsley.

Spinach & Pine Nut Triangles

(Spanakopita)

1 roll filo dough (found in the frozen dessert section in most supermarkets)

2 tbsp olive oil

Olive oil cooking spray

2 cups chopped frozen spinach

1 tbsp sea salt

3 cloves garlic, minced

2 tbsp pine nuts, coarsely mashed

1 cup crumbled feta cheese

Place frozen spinach in microwave-safe container with cover. Defrost spinach just enough to handle and squeeze out excess water. Place drained spinach in a bowl and set aside. In a medium-sized skillet, heat oil over Medium-Low heat. Add garlic and pine nuts. Once garlic and nuts are softened, add spinach and salt. Mix well and cook until heated through. Add feta, mix, then remove from heat.

Coat a large, flat cookie sheet with olive oil cooking spray. Unroll package of filo dough and gently place two sheets on top of each other on cookie sheet. Spray dough with cooking spray generously. Place ¼ cup of spinach mixture along the edge of the filo dough. Roll up, flatten and lie seam down on cookie sheet. Continue with next two sheets of filo dough until all the mixture is gone (should make about 5 rolls).

Arrange rolls on sheets so they don't touch each other. Spray generously with more cooking spray and bake in 350 degree oven for 10 minutes. Turn once and bake another 5-7 minutes, or until well browned on ends and lightly browned in middle. Cool until warm to touch. Cut into small diagonal shapes and arrange on a serving platter. Serve warm.

Pita & Gorgonzola Nachos

1 package pita chips

2½ oz shredded gorgonzola, blue cheese or any other sharp cheese of your liking

¼ cup sweet balsamic vinegar

Spread pita chips in a single flat layer on a cookie sheet. Sprinkle liberally with cheese. Bake at 350 degrees until all the cheese has melted and chips are heated throughout. Splash with balsamic vinegar and serve immediately.

Tangy Yogurt Spread
(Lebni)

Called "lebni" in Lebanon, this low-fat, healthy appetizer is a great substitute for your morning breakfast spread. Instead of using butter, margarine, or cream cheese on your toasted pita, toast, or bagel, use this delicious yogurt spread for a nice change.

1 32 oz container low-fat plain yogurt (avoid using non-fat)

2–3 tsp sea salt (or to taste)

3–4 tbsp olive oil

Place a small colander on top of a bowl that can hold about 1 cup of liquid. Line the colander with two or three bowl shaped paper coffee filters, overlapping them so that all of the holes at the bottom are covered. Empty entire contents of yogurt into colander and cover loosely with a cheese cloth or a clean dish towel. Let sit on counter for 24 hours until all the water has evaporated and the yogurt has a pleasant, tangy taste.*

Serve yogurt on a flat dish, spread flat in a thick layer. Drizzle olive oil and sea salt on top. Decorate by alternating cucumber wheels and pitted calamata olives on the outside of the dish. Serve with pita chips.

* It's perfectly safe to leave the yogurt out without refrigeration for 1–2 days. This is how sour cream and cheeses are made. If you are not comfortable with it, then put it in the refrigerator while the water is being removed. The tangy flavor will be dulled, though! Try leaving it out for 2 days and discover the differences in flavors!

Zesty Lemon Hummus

1 15.5 oz can chickpeas, reserving ½ cup of its juice

2 tbsp olive oil

2 small cloves garlic

2 tbsp tahini paste

The juice of 1 whole, ripe lemon, hand squeezed (or ¼ cup bottled lemon juice)

¼ tsp grated lemon zest

1 dash hot sauce

1 pinch ground cumin

Serve with sliced red onions or scallions and fresh, chopped parsley on the side.

Process all ingredients in food processor or blender until smooth. Store in refrigerator. Serve cold or at room temperature with fresh pita wedges or toasted pita chips. You can also serve with sliced red onions, scallions or fresh, chopped parsley on the side.

Quick Homemade Salsa

There have been plenty of nights when my husband or kids are in the mood for some salsa and I have none in the house. One evening, when I had just the basics on hand, I made some on the fly and the result was delicious!

1 can stewed tomatoes, drained & coarsely chopped

¼ cup loosely packed fresh cilantro, chopped

½ tsp sugar

¼ cup yellow or Vidalia onion, finely chopped

2 dashes hot sauce (or to taste)

Add the following optional ingredients to your salsa:
fresh or bottled lime juice
¼ cup black beans, well drained
¼ cup canned corn, well drained

Coarsely chop the tomatoes, or mash lightly with a potato masher, and add the rest of the ingredients. Mix well. Ready to serve immediately at room temperature, or place in an airtight container and store in refrigerator until ready to serve. Serve with tortilla chips.

Bill's Salsa

My dear friend Bill is one of my best critics and an excellent cook. He's not a big fan of chunky salsa and prefers a pureed version. He and his wife, Ellen made this for me and my husband Ron one night and it was truly the best salsa I've ever had.

1 14.5 oz can of diced tomato (flavored with sweet onion), well drained

1 small onion chopped

2 cloves of garlic

1 tbsp of fresh cilantro, chopped

1 tbsp of hot peppers, chopped (found jarred in most grocery stores)

1 tsp of sugar

Cumin to taste

Salt and Pepper to taste

Place all ingredients in a blender or food processor and blend until slightly pureed. Serve chilled with tortilla chips or your favorite Mexican dish.

❋ Crock Pot Recipes ❋

Although the crock pot was never used in my family growing up, as a working mother, I have learned to love it!. Over the years I have adapted some of the traditional Mediterranean meals into easy, low-prep crock pot meals. A far cry from the same ole same ole crock pot dishes.

I usually prepare crock pot meals the night before. After I put all of the ingredients in the pot, I cover it and place the insert in the refrigerator overnight. In the morning before leaving for work, I simply put the pot in its sleeve and set it on Low. And the best part? Dinner's ready by the time you get home from work!

Ideas for your picky eater:

Serve plain pasta, pour soup stock over it, straining out the vegetables. Your kids will still get the nutrition of the vegetables from the broth. Serve with crusty bread. My son tops it off with Goldfish® or Saltine® crackers.

Anna's Minestrone Soup

My Italian mother and Grandmother both cooked this soup often. It's usually a quick meal to prepare*, but it's even quicker when using your crock pot. No sautéing is necessary.

¼ cup olive oil

2 large cloves garlic, minced

1 large onion, diced

1 28 oz can chopped stewed tomatoes with juice (or two 15.5 oz cans) (You can use 1 28 oz can crushed tomatoes, adding a full can of water to the stew).

6 cups beef, chicken, or vegetable broth

1 10- or 12-oz pkg of frozen mixed vegetables (or a combination of pearl onions, carrots and green beans)

1 15.5 oz can red kidney beans, fully drained

1 15.5 oz can chickpeas, fully drained

¼ cup loosely packed fresh parsley, chopped

1 tbsp fresh oregano, chopped (or 1 tsp dried)

1 tbsp fresh basil, chopped (or 1 tsp dried)

1 tbsp sea salt (or to taste)

1 tsp fresh ground pepper (or to taste)

1 bay leaf

⅛ tsp crushed red pepper flakes (optional)

½ lb small pasta such as ditalini or elbow macaroni, cooked and set aside

¼ cup grated parmasean cheese

Place all ingredients, except for pasta, in crock pot. Add add'l drinking water if necessary to fully cover the vegetables. Cook on Low for 7–8 hours, or on High for 3–4 hours. Add cooked pasta just prior to serving. Mix well and sprinkle with add'l parmesan cheese. Serve with crusty bread.

* You can follow the recipe above for the stove top by sautéing the onion and garlic in olive oil on Medium-Low heat. Once softened, add the rest of the ingredients. Bring to a boil and simmer for 20 minutes if using stewed tomatoes, 40 minutes or longer using crushed tomatoes. You can also add uncooked pasta with a bit more water in the last 10 minutes of the cooking time. Serve when pasta is cooked to your liking and add fresh parmesan cheese.

Mluhea in a Crock Pot

(Mediterranean Chicken & Garlic Stew)

My Sito (Grandmother in Arabic) would roll over in her grave if she knew I was preparing an 8-hour prep time meal in under 20 minutes! This dish is one of my favorite Mediterranean meals. It used to take so long to prepare, and the Mluhea was often difficult to find in the United States, so we were lucky to have this meal once a year. Mluhea is in the spinach family. It's very similar to Swiss chard. You can use either Swiss chard or chopped spinach if you can't get your hands on Mluhea, which is only found in Middle Eastern Stores. If you happen to find Mluhea, avoid the dried variety and buy it frozen.

I have one warning: Prepare yourself! This dish is loaded with garlic, Lebanese spices, and topped with a wonderfully sharp and salty condiment—red onion marinated in red wine vinegar. This special occasion dish can now be a weekly favorite in your house.

½ head of fresh garlic, peeled and minced using a garlic press

1 bunch fresh Swiss Chard, washed and chopped *or* 1 large package frozen chopped spinach (*about 20–24 oz*)

1 bunch fresh cilantro leaves, chopped (including the tender part of the stem)

1 lb uncooked chicken, diced

1 tsp black pepper

2 tsp sea salt

1 tsp Mediterranean Spice Mix*

6 cups low sodium chicken stock *plus* additional broth or water as necessary for a soup consistency

2–3 large pieces of Lebanese bread, (or 5 or 6 small pita pockets) cut in half from the seam, and toasted to a crisp in an oven or toaster.

Ideas for your picky eater:

In a flat dish, serve the plain rice, crusty bread and slices of chicken from the soup. Serve with your child's favorite condiment (i.e. sweet & sour sauce, ketchup, or ranch dressing).

*Mediterranean Spice Mix:

- 1 tbsp allspice
- ½ tsp cinnamon
- ½ tsp nutmeg
- ¼ tsp turmeric
- ¼ tsp ground cloves

Keep on hand in an airtight container. Use this spice mix to add a Mediterranean flare to any chicken, vegetable or beef dish.

Continues

1 cup cooked white or brown rice (save for later)

½ large red onion, diced

1 cup red wine vinegar

While you are preparing the rest of the ingredients, toast the Lebanese bread directly on rack of 350 degree oven for 3–4 minutes, then turn over and bake another 3–4 minutes until very crispy, but not burned. Take bread out of oven and let cool. Once cool, break into large bite-sized pieces. Place in an airtight container until ready to serve.

Prepare the rice for cooking. I find that using the microwave saves me time. Place 1 cup rice and 2 cups water in microwaveable bowl with salt and a little butter or margarine. Cook covered for 5 minutes on High power. Once the 5 minutes are up, cover loosely, allowing a little air so water doesn't boil over, and cook on 50% power for 15 minutes.

Heat 2 tbsp olive oil in a large skillet on Medium heat. Add minced garlic and chopped cilantro and stir constantly until the garlic is soft, but not brown and cilantro is moist and mixed well with garlic. Place the garlic/cilantro mixture in crock pot, add other ingredients* (except for toasted bread, rice and condiments), and cook on Low for 7–8 hours, or on High for 4–5 hours.

To serve, use individual soup bowls lined with 1 cup toasted bread, then add 1 ladle of cooked rice, followed by the soup stock and several tablespoons chopped red onion and vinegar. Some like to use more or less of the red onion condiment; I use about ½ cup!

You've learned from your grandmother that chicken soup is a cure for the common cold, but this meal is sure to cure any ailment!

* Be sure to add more chicken broth or water as necessary to cover all ingredients for a soup consistency.

Nonnie's Pasta Fazool

2 15.5 oz cans cannellini beans with juice

2 tbsp flour

2 tbsp olive oil

1–2 cloves garlic, minced

1 large onion, chopped

2 stalks celery, chopped with leaves

2 med carrots, peeled and chopped

1 28 oz can diced stewed tomatoes with juice

¼ cup parsley, chopped

2 cubes beef bullion

2 tsp salt

¼ tsp pepper

1 tbsp dried basil

½ cup uncooked small pasta, like elbows, ditalini, etc.

Drinking water

Fresh parmesan cheese (optional)

Make a roux with flour and ¼ cup water. Place all ingredients in crock pot* including uncooked pasta. Add enough water so that all ingredients are covered, then add ½ cup more. Cover and cook for 6–8 hours on Low, or 4–5 hours on High.

Remove ½ of the stew with a ladle and place in a blender or food processor. Blend until smooth and pour back into pot with the rest of the stew.** Stir to thicken slightly. Adjust seasonings according to taste. Serve with fresh parmesan cheese and crusty bread.

Ideas for your picky eater:

To satisfy your picky eaters and to enjoy a more "al dente" pasta, cook separately from rest of ingredients. Serve bowls of plain pasta and drizzle with juice from the fazool. Top with parmesan cheese.

*For stovetop method, sauté onion and garlic in olive oil until softened. Follow first two steps, bring pot to a boil, and then simmer 20–30 minutes, stirring occasionally.

**If you don't want to pull out your blender or food processor, simply use a potato masher, mash a little of the bean mixture and stir to thicken slightly.

Chicken & Spinach Stew

Ideas for your picky eater:

My daughter would rather do without the spinach, so I separate it from the diced chicken and serve with raw carrots and celery with ranch dressing on the side.

This is one of the quickest meals I have ever prepared. Prep time is just 5 minutes and it's got three basic food groups all in one meal!

1 lb uncooked chicken, diced

2 tbsp olive oil

2 cloves garlic, minced

1 small package frozen chopped spinach

1 small white or yellow onion, diced

½ cup long grain rice (white, brown, wild or an exotic blend of all three)*, *uncooked*

1 15.5 oz can chicken broth (I prefer low sodium)

Salt and pepper (to taste)

½ tsp each dried oregano and basil

Water to fill crock pot and/or cover all ingredients.

Place all ingredients in crock pot. Cook for 7–8 hours on Low or 4–5 hours on High.

If the crockpot isn't an option, try placing everything in a large pot on the stovetop and simmer for 15 minutes, or until chicken is cooked through.

*Choose a slow-cooking rice and not one that has been partially cooked. Some kinds of rice cook too quickly for the crock pot and may become over cooked. You may choose to cook the rice separately and use less water in the stew.

Aunt Lee's Marinara Sauce

In the past, I used to try all kinds of fancy spices and other ingredients to make my marinara sauce more flavorful. However, it never was quite right. My Aunt Lee is an excellent traditional Italian cook and she was more than willing to share her secrets with me. And now I will share them with you. This basic marinara sauce is so simple and quick, you won't believe just how good it is. Sometimes going back to the basics is a reminder to keep it simple!

3 tbsp olive oil

2 large cloves garlic, minced

2 28 oz cans crushed tomatoes

1 cup water

1 medium yellow onion, diced

1 large carrot, peeled and cut into 3 pieces

1 large celery stick, cut into 3 pieces

Salt and ground black pepper (to taste)

2 tbsp fresh flat leaf parsley, chopped (or 2 tsp dried)

2 tbsp fresh basil, chopped (or 2 tsp dried)

2 tsp sugar or 2 tbsp red wine (to cut the acidity)

Place all ingredients in a crock pot.* Cook for 7–8 hours on Low, or 4–5 hours on High. Discard the carrot and celery before serving.

*For stovetop directions, combine all ingredients in a Dutch oven or large stewing pot. Bring to a boil and simmer covered for 1 hour, stirring occasionally.

Piccata in a Crock Pot

You can prepare this meal in the morning, just 10 minutes before leaving for work.

1 lb boneless breast of chicken (if frozen, use whole pieces or cut into strips if thawed)

2 cloves garlic, minced

2 tbsp olive oil

¼ cup loosely packed fresh flat leaf Italian parsley, chopped (or 2 tsp dried)

1 tsp fresh chopped basil, (or ½ tsp dried)

2 cups chicken broth

1 tbsp flour or corn starch

1 can quartered artichoke hearts and its juice

3 tbsp capers, well rinsed

2 tbsp fresh or bottled lemon juice

Sea salt and pepper (to taste)

Place the oil, minced garlic and fresh herbs in the crock pot and set on High while preparing the rest of the ingredients. Mix occasionally so the flavors blend well. Keep on High for about 5 minutes before adding the remaining ingredients. Add chicken and mix well, making sure that the chicken gets rubbed in with the herbs. Add salt, pepper, artichoke hearts with juice, capers, lemon juice and mix well. Make a roux with some of the chicken broth and flour, then add the rest of chicken broth and roux to crock pot. Cover and cook for 7–8 hours on Low, or keep on High for 4 hours. Serve with cooked pasta or rice.

Lemony Lentil Soup

This is one of my favorite family soups and it's just as easy to make on the stovetop* as it is in the crock pot.

2 tbsp olive oil

2 stalks celery, diced

1 large carrot, diced

1 15.5 oz can stewed tomatoes and its juice

2–3 cloves fresh garlic, minced

1 small white or yellow onion, diced

1 lb lentils, rinsed

½ cup good quality lemon juice (use more or less depending on taste)

2 quarts beef broth (or 2 quarts water with two cubes beef bullion)

Salt and pepper (to taste)

½ tsp each dried oregano and basil

3 medium sized potatoes, peeled and diced into bite sized pieces

Add'l drinking water to fill crock pot and/or cover all ingredients.

Place all ingredients in crock pot. Cook for 7–8 hours on Low or 4–5 hours on High.

* For stovetop preparation, sauté olive oil, celery, garlic and onions. Add dried spices and cook for one minute. Add remaining ingredients. Cover and bring to a boil. Simmer for 40 minutes until lentils and potatoes are fully cooked and soft to the bite.

The following recipes are some of our family's favorites. They are also the ones most enjoyed by friends. We have improvised the traditional cooking methods to make all of the meals quick and easy for today's family.

Basic Sauté

I have a basic sauté recipe that can be used as the foundation for a variety of meals. From a chicken & mushroom dish, seafood sauté, to a veal or chicken piccata, this Basic Sauté is always the start of something good.

¼ cup olive oil
2 large cloves garlic, minced
½ cup broth (chicken, beef or vegetable), clam juice or white wine
½ tsp sea salt
1 tbsp fresh flat leaf Italian parsley, chopped (or 1 tsp dried)
1 tbsp fresh basil, chopped (or 1 tsp dried)
Freshly ground pepper (to taste)
Pinch of dried crushed red pepper flakes (optional)

Heat olive oil in large skillet over Medium-Low heat. Add the parsley, basil, salt, pepper and crushed red pepper. Cook until flavors are infused (about 2–3 minutes). Add minced garlic and cook for about 30 seconds, being careful not to burn or overcook. Add broth and simmer for about 5 minutes. Stir well and remove from heat in preparation for whatever meal you are about to cook.

Add this basic sauté to sautéed chicken, pan seared fish, or to cooked pasta. See the following recipes for complete instructions.

Sautéed Chicken, Mushroom & Artichoke

Try using dried porcini or crimini mushrooms for a variety of flavors. Follow instructions on mushroom package to properly hydrate and remove sediment.

Substitute the liquid for some of the chicken broth for an enhanced mushroom flavor!

If you make this dish a few times, you will find how quick and easy it can be with practice. I often make this meal during the week in under 20 minutes.

Basic Sauté:

¼ cup olive oil

2 large cloves garlic, minced

½ cup chicken broth

1 tbsp fresh flat leaf Italian parsley, chopped (or 1 tsp dried)

1 tsp fresh chopped basil, (or ½ tsp dried)

Freshly ground pepper (to taste)

½ tsp sea salt (or to taste)

Pinch of dried crushed red pepper flakes (optional)

Remaining Ingredients:

1 tbsp non-hydrogenated margarine

¼ cup dry white wine or additional chicken broth

1 small pkg fresh sliced mushrooms, any kind (Note: You will get different results with each variety of mushroom.)

1 15.5 oz can quartered artichoke hearts and ½ of its juice (reserve the remaining liquid)

1 lb boneless, skinless chicken breasts, cut in large cubes or strips, or chicken tenderloins, trimmed and uncut

¼ cup flour

½ cup loosely packed fresh flat leaf parsley, chopped

Salt and pepper (to taste)

2 cups cooked white or brown rice or ½ lb cooked pasta (optional)

Continues

Begin cooking the rice or pasta (if you plan on serving it with this dish). While the pasta is boiling or the rice is cooking, prepare the rest of the meal.

In a large skillet, melt the butter or margarine over Medium-High heat. Add the sliced mushrooms and a sprinkle of salt and pepper and stir well. When the mushrooms look like they have absorbed all of the butter and begin to sizzle quite a bit, add the white wine. Let cook uncovered for a few minutes, or until some of the liquid has evaporated. Stir occasionally. Place the mushroom mixture in a dish and set aside for later use.

Place the flour in a deep bowl. Coat the chicken with flour on both sides. Keep the chicken in the flour bowl until you are ready to use it.

Remove any bits of mushroom left over in the skillet and put the skillet back on burner over Medium-High heat. Add 3 tbsp olive oil. When the skillet is hot, add the chicken and brown for approximately 1–2 minutes on each side. Once the chicken is browned on both sides, add the Basic Sauté ingredients and stir until all spices and garlic are well blended. Add the can of artichoke hearts and ½ of its juice, the cooked mushrooms, parsley and more salt and fresh ground pepper. Bring to a light boil, gently stir, then lower heat to a simmer and cover. Cook for 5–7 minutes or until the chicken is cooked through and the sauce has thickened to your liking. If serving over pasta, I suggest adding the rest of the artichoke juice or chicken broth to create a "loose" sauce. Do not add more wine at this point, since the alcohol flavor will be too strong.

For a thicker sauce, make a roux, by adding ¼ cup of the sauce in a small cup with 1 tablespoon flour or corn starch. Whisk until smooth and add to the sauce. Taste and adjust seasonings as necessary.

Pour over rice or pasta, or serve alone. Great with broccoli or spinach as a side dish (See pages 75–83 for a complete listing of side dishes).

Seafood Sauté—Spanish Style

This is a very quick meal that's accented with wonderful Spanish flavors.

¼ cup olive oil

2 cloves garlic, minced

¼ tsp cumin

¼ tsp oregano

A pinch of red pepper flakes (optional)

Fresh ground black pepper (to taste)

1 cup clam juice

2 tsp Cilantro soup base (found in the Spanish or Mexican isle in most
   grocery stores)

The juice of 2 limes (or ¼ cup bottled lime juice)

2 6.5 oz cans minced clams (reserving its juice for later use)

½ lb fresh or frozen white, flaky fish

1 handful frozen, peeled shrimp

2 tbsp flour

2 cups cooked Spanish rice (see page 76 for recipe)

Heat oil in large skillet over Medium-High heat. Coat white fish with the flour
and pan sear, browning on both sides. Turn only once. As soon as fish has
been turned over to brown second side, add the cumin, oregano, red pepper
flakes and minced garlic. Stir constantly alongside the fish, moving the garlic
and spices around to avoid burning. After a few seconds, add lime juice,
clam juice, cilantro base, and black pepper. Cover and cook on High until
liquid comes to a boil. Reduce heat and simmer. Immediately add clams and
shrimp, using some of the clam juice if more liquid is necessary. Cover again
and simmer until shrimp turns pink. Serve immediately over Spanish, plain or
brown rice.

10-Minute Fra Diavlo

You're not going to believe how quickly you can get this meal on the table! It's also great for those surprise guests that enjoy Italian and seafood dishes!

Basic Sauté:

> ¼ cup olive oil
>
> 2 cloves garlic, minced
>
> ¼ cup loosely packed fresh parsley (or 1 tbsp dried)
>
> 2 tbsp fresh basil, chopped (or 1 tsp each dried)
>
> Sea salt and fresh ground black pepper (to taste)
>
> ⅛ tsp dried crushed red pepper flakes (or to taste)

6–8 cups Aunt Lee's Simple Marinara Sauce (see page 33 for recipe) (or your favorite jarred spaghetti sauce)

½ lb fresh or frozen flaky fish (such as haddock or cod)

1 large handful frozen raw shrimp, peeled

1 6.5 oz can minced clams and its juice (fresh clams are better if you have the time to purchase & cook that day)

1 4 oz bottle clam juice

Fresh ground black pepper (to taste)

Add'l fresh crushed red pepper flakes (optional)

¼ cup light cream or half and half (optional for a pink Diavlo sauce)

1 lb cooked linguini or thick spaghetti (you can use any thick pasta you have on hand, such as rigatoni or ziti)

While you are boiling the water to cook the pasta, prepare the Basic Sauté by heating a large skillet with olive oil over Medium heat. Add minced garlic, fresh herbs, salt, pepper and crushed red pepper and mix well. Cook for about 30 seconds, being careful not burn the garlic.

Add the marinara sauce and bring to a simmer. Add all seafood and clam juice. Cook for 3–4 minutes, or until shrimp turns pink and the fish is cooked through. Add additional seasonings as needed. Serve over pasta.

Ideas for your picky eater:

Avoid adding the extra crushed red pepper to the sauté pan and put it on individual servings. Strain the seafood and pour plain sauce over pasta. If your kids eat some, but not all seafood (as my daughter does) serve pieces of the flaky fish, for example, on a separate dish and squeeze fresh lemon on top.

Many traditional Italian cooks would never top a fish dish with parmesan cheese or add cream to a Diavlo sauce. I say, do what you think tastes good and what your family would like! Enjoy!

For your picky eater:

Place a scoop of plain pasta in a dish and use a slotted spoon to strain the clams. I use only the juice for my son who could do without the clams.

Linguini and Clam Sauce

My entire family loves this meal. It's very quick to prepare and very little ingredients are needed. By the time the pasta is done cooking—dinner is served!

Basic Sauté:

½ cup olive oil

2–3 cloves garlic, minced

¼ cup loosely packed fresh flat leaf Italian parsley, chopped (or 2 tsp dried)

1 tbsp fresh basil, chopped (or 1 tsp dried)

Sea salt and fresh ground black pepper (to taste)

⅛ tsp dried crushed red pepper flakes (or to taste)

¼ cup bottled clam juice

2 cans minced clams with juice

1 lb linguini or spaghetti

Bring a large pot of water to boil and cook pasta according to package instructions. While the water is getting ready to boil, heat olive oil in a large frying pan on Medium-High heat. Add the dried spices, salt and pepper and cook until flavors are infused. Lower heat and add minced garlic. Cook until garlic has softened, but not burned. Add bottled clam juice, canned clams and its juice. Bring to a slow simmer and turn off burner once clams are heated through. Be careful not to overcook the clams, or they will become rubbery.

Once linguini is cooked, drain *slightly*, leaving a bit of water in with the pasta. Pour some of the clam sauce over the pasta so it won't stick. Serve immediately in individual bowls, topping with more clam sauce and a side of crusty bread.*

* Traditional Italian cooks would never approve of putting grated cheese in a meal with fish, but boy does it taste good in this dish!

Tandoori Chicken

This is an Indian recipe that I make often because it's quick, there's only a few ingredients and it's quite yummy! The flavors are more enhanced if you can marinate it overnight, so try to prepare this the night before.

1 lb boneless chicken breast, fat trimmed and cut into large, bite sized pieces

2 cups chopped fresh or frozen spinach (if frozen, defrost and squeeze out excess water)

Marinade:

2 tbsp olive oil

½ cup plain low-fat yogurt (avoid fat free)

2 large cloves of garlic, minced

2 tbsp fresh squeezed lemon juice (or 4 tbsp bottled)

1½ tbsp Indian Spice Mix*

* **Indian Spice Mix:**
Keep on hand in an air tight container a combination of the following spices:

- 1 tbsp ground cumin
- 1 tsp ground coriander
- ½ tsp cayenne pepper
- ½ tsp dried ground ginger
- ½ tsp ground cloves
- ½ tsp fresh ground black pepper
- 1 tsp salt

Preheat oven to 350 degrees. Combine all marinade items in a medium sized bowl. Lightly salt the cut chicken pieces and place in marinade. Add the chopped spinach. Mix well and cover. Place in refrigerator overnight or marinate for an hour if possible.

Place the chicken mixture, including all of the marinade, in a single layer in an ovenproof baking dish. Bake uncovered for 20 minutes, then broil on highest oven rack on High heat for 7–10 minutes, or until the chicken turns slightly brown and is fully cooked.

Serve with Mediterranean or Indian rice (pages 75 and 77).

Your Pantry's House Stew

The good thing about stew is that as long as you have the basics, you can be creative when you haven't been to the store in a bit and need to work with what you have on hand.*

4 tbsp olive oil

1 medium onion (white, yellow, or Vidalia), chopped

2 large cloves garlic, minced

2 cups chicken, beef or vegetable broth

½ lb cubed chicken or stewing beef, uncooked

2 tbsp flour or cornstarch and water to make a roux

Any kind of stewing vegetable(s): (carrots, celery, green beans, etc.)

3 small potatoes, peeled and diced (or 1 cup rice, uncooked)

1 14.5 oz can stewed tomatoes with its juice

1 tbsp each fresh or ½ tsp each dried herbs (parsley & basil, or thyme & rosemary, and celery salt if you don't have celery)

2 cups fresh or frozen green leafy vegetable(s) (spinach, escarole, or Swiss chard)

1 Bay leaf

Salt and pepper (to taste)

Pinch of red pepper flakes (optional)

Heat 3 tbsp olive oil in large pot. Add chicken or beef and sprinkle with salt and flour. Cook on all sides until slightly browned. Add onion, garlic and spices and sauté until translucent, adding 1 tbsp additional olive oil if needed. Add remaining ingredients. Add enough water to just cover everything. Bring to boil and simmer, covered for one hour. Adjust seasonings and add more broth or water for a thinner consistency, or make a roux with flour and stewing liquid for a thicker consistency. Serve with fresh, crusty Italian or sourdough bread.

* Also a good crockpot recipe!

White Chili

This recipe was given to me by a co-worker years ago. She is a fabulous cook and knows a good recipe when she sees one. The original recipe was found on the back of a spice company's label. She modified it quite a bit. I have made some adjustments to it as well to make one of my most popular dishes. It is such a big hit with friends and family that I was encouraged to share it.

The Quick Version—Serves 2–4

3 tbsp olive oil

1 medium onion, diced

2 small cloves garlic

1 tsp oregano

1/8 tsp dried red pepper

1/2 tsp cumin

1 cup chicken broth

1 4.25 oz can chopped green chilies, with juice

1 lb uncooked boneless, skinless chicken breast, cut into bite sized pieces

1 15.5 oz can white kidney (cannellini) beans, with juice

1 15.5 oz can chickpeas, drained

1/4 cup loosely packed fresh cilantro leaves, chopped

Salt and ground black pepper (to taste)

Tortilla chips

Grated cheddar cheese, sour cream and/or additional cilantro for garnish

Sauté onions in oil until translucent (about 5 min). Add the garlic and dried spices and sauté for a few minutes more. Add stock and canned chilies and simmer for 10 minutes. Add chicken, beans (both cannellini and chickpeas), and cilantro; simmer for approximately 10 minutes, or until the chicken is cooked through. Adjust seasonings to taste. Garnish lightly with additional toppings and serve with Tortilla chips.

Continues

White Chili (continued)

This is for when you are entertaining a larger crowd and you have the time to prepare the night before.

Serves 6–8

1 whole chicken (poach in water with salt the way you would for anything else requiring cooked chicken, and *reserve* 4 cups of the liquid)

4 tbsp olive oil

1 large or 2 medium sized onions, diced

3 cloves garlic

2 tsp oregano

1 tsp dried red pepper

1 tsp cumin

2 4.25 oz cans chopped green chilies, with its juice

1 large (28 oz) can of white kidney beans, (cannellini) with its juice

1 15.5 oz can of chickpeas, drained

½ cup loosely packed fresh cilantro leaves, chopped

Salt and ground pepper (to taste)

Tortilla chips

Grated cheddar cheese, sour cream and/or additional cilantro for garnish

The night before or morning of, poach the chicken in boiling water for about one hour seasoning the water with sea salt. Cool the poached chicken enough for you to pull the meat off the bones. Shred into bite-sized pieces and set aside. Sauté onions in oil until translucent (about 5 minutes). Add the garlic and dried spices and sauté a few minutes more. Add stock and canned chilies, simmer for 10 minutes, then add the beans (both cannellini and chickpeas) and cilantro and cook for an additional 10 minutes. Add the chicken and as much of the reserved cooking liquid as you need for a good consistency. Adjust seasonings to taste. Garnish lightly with additional toppings and serve with tortilla chips.

Escarole and Beans with Sausage

1 lb sweet Italian or spicy sausage, cut into bite sized pieces

2 15.5 oz cans cannellini beans with juice

½ lb ditalini pasta, uncooked

½ tsp each dried basil and oregano (use fresh if you have them!)

Dash of crushed red pepper flakes (optional)

Sea salt and fresh ground black pepper (to taste)

2–3 cloves garlic, minced

3 tbsp olive oil

1 bunch fresh escarole, washed thoroughly and torn into pieces

4 cups cold water with 2 chicken bullion cubes or 2 tsp chicken paste (or 4 cups chicken broth)

In a medium sized frying pan sauté chopped sausage in olive oil over Medium heat. Once browned, lower heat and add garlic and herbs. Sauté for about a minute, being careful not to burn the garlic. Add the cracked pepper, the beans with its juice, and broth. Bring to a boil for 1–2 minutes, then reduce heat to a slow simmer and cook 5–10 minutes.

Add escarole and turn up the heat slightly (but not to boiling), and simmer for about 20 minutes, or until escarole leaves are tender. Add dry pasta 10 minutes before serving and cook until tender.* Serve immediately.

Season to taste with salt and cracked pepper.

* Pasta tends to get overcooked if cooked too long in the stew. It absorbs much of the liquid, leaving a thicker texture. If you plan on having leftovers, a good idea is to cook the pasta separately and add to the stew just minutes before serving.

*Mediterranean Spice Mix:

- **1 tbsp allspice**
- **½ tsp cinnamon**
- **½ tsp nutmeg**
- **¼ tsp turmeric**
- **¼ tsp ground cloves.**

Keep on hand in an airtight container. Use this spice mix to add a Mediterranean flare to any chicken, vegetable or beef dish.

Veggie Burgers

(Falafel)

You can make the patties a few days in advance to save you time during a busy work week.

2 cups frozen green peas, fully thawed

1 15.5 oz can chick peas, fully drained

2 cloves of garlic, crushed

¾–1 cup plain bread crumbs

2 tbsp olive oil

1 small onion, chopped

¼ cup fresh cilantro, chopped

¼ cup fresh parsley, chopped

1 tbsp ground cumin

1 tbsp Mediterranean Spice Mix*

Salt and pepper (to taste)

Lightly squeeze excess water out of the green peas with your hand, and place in a food processor. Add all remaining ingredients, *except for bread crumbs and olive oil*, in the food processor and blend until you get a soft dough-like mixture. Remove and place in large bowl and add the olive oil. Knead in bread crumbs, adding a bit at a time until you get a workable doughy mixture. Divide and shape the mixture into small patties.

Coat a large fry pan with enough olive oil to cover the bottom well. Fry each side on Medium High heat until dark brown. With a slotted spatula remove patties and place on a flat dish lined with paper towels to drain some of the oil.

Serve warm, rolled in pita bread, with lettuce, tomatoes and Tarator if desired (see next page for recipe). You can also serve on a hamburger bun with mayo, pickles, tomatoes and lettuce.

Continues

Tarator Sauce:

¼ cup tahini (sesame seed paste)

½ cup lemon juice
    1 tablespoon water

2 cloves garlic, crushed

½ tsp salt

1 tbsp fresh flat leaf parsley, finely chopped

Pinch of cumin

In a food processor, combine tahini, garlic, lemon juice, salt, and cumin together. Mix well and add water as you are combining the ingredients. Transfer to small bowl. Stir in parsley. Serve with Falafel burgers as a toping. Store unused portion in refrigerator for up to a week in an airtight container.

For your picky eater:

My kids love these vegetarian burgers! Instead of the Tarator sauce, they dip their veggie burgers in ketchup.

Getting my son to try and enjoy something other than pasta, PBJ and hot dogs was quite the victory for me!

Mediterranean Gumbo

For variety, add cooked sausage, like chorizo or linguica, and/or stewing beef or lamb to this dish to create a fantastic one pot meal for your family and friends.

This is another dish I discovered when I craved a vegetarian meal and used whatever was left in my pantry. It's also a unique side to complement any beef, chicken or lamb dish.

1 10 oz package frozen cut okra

1 cup frozen chopped spinach

½ cup frozen French cut green beans

4 tbsp olive oil

1 cup Spanish or Vidalia onion, chopped

2 cloves garlic, minced

¼ tsp ground cumin

¼ tsp ground allspice

⅛ tsp ground turmeric

⅛ tsp crushed red pepper flakes (to taste)

Sea salt and fresh ground pepper (to taste)

1 15.5 oz can chickpeas, drained

½ cup stewed tomatoes, slightly drained

1 cup white or brown rice, uncooked

2 cups water

1 tsp vegetable soup base (or 1 cube vegetable bullion)

Fresh parsley, chopped

Sauté onions and garlic in olive oil on Medium-High heat. Lower heat to Medium and add okra. Cook for about 2 minutes, or until okra softens. Add spices and sauté a few minutes more. Add spinach, green beans and the remaining ingredients.

Bring to boil then simmer, covered, until rice is cooked (about 20 minutes).

Meat Pies

(Fatayer)

In the past, my grandparents used to make the dough for these Meat Pies from scratch. Now, you can just purchase pizza dough at your local supermarket. Or for some decadently sinful flavor, use your favorite brand of refrigerated crescent roll dough.

1 ball of dough, kneaded and ready for use (or 1 pkg crescent roll dough, rolled out with seams closed)

½ lb lean ground lamb or sirloin

1 small onion, chopped

1 cup plain lowfat yogurt (using lebni instead is IDEAL for a nice tangy flavor, see page 23)

Salt and pepper (to taste)

¼ cup fresh parsley, chopped (or ½ tsp dried)

½ tsp dried mint

½ tsp Mediterranean Spice Mix*

½ cup pine nuts

2 tbsp olive oil

White flour (to keep on hand in case dough becomes too moist to close up crust)

Preheat oven to 400 degrees.

Combine all ingredients above, except for dough, to create filling. Knead well with hands and squeeze out any excess liquid from filling.

Roll dough into 6" rounds, like a pie crust. Place approximately 2 table-spoons of filling on each crust round and close in the shape of a triangle. Be careful not to get juices on the edges of the crust, as this will make it diffi-cult to crimp shut. If this happens, dip fingers in flour to avoid sticking. Cover the bottom of a baking tray with oil and place pies in rows. Lightly brush with olive oil and bake until golden brown (about 25–30 minutes).

*Mediterranean Spice Mix:

- **1 tbsp allspice**
- **½ tsp cinnamon**
- **½ tsp nutmeg**
- **¼ tsp turmeric**
- **¼ tsp ground cloves**

Keep on hand in an airtight container. Use this spice mix to add a Mediterranean flare to any chicken, vegetable or beef dish.

Spinach Pies

(Spinach Fatayer)

***Mediterranean
Spice Mix:**

- 1 tbsp allspice
- ½ tsp cinnamon
- ½ tsp nutmeg
- ¼ tsp turmeric
- ¼ tsp ground cloves.

**Keep on hand in an
airtight container. Use
this spice mix to add a
Mediterranean flare to
any chicken, vegetable or
beef dish.**

1 ball of dough, kneaded and ready for use (or 1 pkg crescent roll dough, rolled out with seams closed)

1 48 oz package fresh or frozen chopped spinach (if frozen, defrost enough to squeeze excess water out)

½ cup fresh lemon juice (or bottled)

1 large onion, finely chopped

1 tsp salt

1 pinch of ground black pepper

1 tsp Mediterranean Spice Mix*

3 tbsp olive oil

If using fresh spinach, wash thoroughly, drain water and remove roots and yellow leaves. Chop well. Combine all ingredients above, *except for dough and olive oil,* to create filling. Knead well with hands and squeeze out any excess liquid from filling. Add 1 tbsp of the olive oil. Mix well again.

Roll dough into 6" rounds, like a pie crust. Place approximately 3 table-spoons of filling on each crust round and close in the shape of a triangle. Be careful not to get juices on the edges of the crust, as this will make it difficult to crimp shut. If this happens, dip fingers in flour to avoid sticking. Cover the bottom of a baking tray with the remaining oil and place pies in rows. Lightly brush with olive oil and bake until golden brown (about 25–30 minutes).

Mediterranean Meatloaf

(Kibbie)

1 lb lean ground beef or lamb

½ cup fine- to medium-grade bulgar (cracked wheat)

1 medium onion, minced

½ cup pine nuts (also known as pignoli nuts) or chopped walnuts

1 tbsp fresh flat leaf parsley, chopped OR 2 tsp dried parsley

2 tbsp water

1 tbsp olive oil

½ tsp sea salt

1 tsp Mediterranean Spice Mix*

¼ tsp hot sauce (optional)

Preheat oven to 350 degrees.

Put pine nuts or walnuts in a plastic baggie and gently pound just to break them up a bit.

Combine the meat, bulgar, minced onion, 1 tablespoon of the olive oil, water, hot sauce (optional), and spices. Knead well with hands until fully blended. Lightly oil an 8 inch square baking dish with 1 tsp of the olive oil. Pat half of the meat mixture into the pan and sprinkle with nuts**, then cover with the remaining meat. Press firmly down, ensuring an even surface. While still in the pan, cut the Kibbie into 1 inch square or diamond shapes, by taking a sharp knife and cutting diagonally in one direction and then again in another direction.

Brush the remaining olive oil over the top and bake for 30–35 minutes, or until firm and browned well. Serve with plain yogurt, Greek yogurt or Lebni (see page 23 for recipe).

Mediterranean Spice Mix:

- 1 tbsp allspice
- ½ tsp cinnamon
- ½ tsp nutmeg
- ¼ tsp turmeric
- ¼ tsp ground cloves

Keep on hand in an airtight container. Use this spice mix to add a Mediterranean flare to any chicken, vegetable or beef dish.

For a lighter meal option, try this dish using ground turkey. Just omit the water, as turkey is more moist than ground beef.

** For a more traditional Kibbe, prepare the stuffing by sautéing in 2 tbsp olive oil, ¼ cup minced onion, a bit of the beef, and pine nuts. Add salt and add'l spices and cook until onion has softened. Place in the middle between meat layers. Follow cooking time above.

Shish Tawook

(Lebanese Barbecued Chicken)

***Mediterranean
Spice Mix:**

- **1 tbsp allspice**
- **½ tsp cinnamon**
- **½ tsp nutmeg**
- **¼ tsp turmeric**
- **¼ tsp ground cloves**

Keep on hand in an airtight container. Use this spice mix to add a Mediterranean flare to any chicken, vegetable or beef dish.

1 lb boneless breast of chicken, fat trimmed and cut into large chunks

3 tbsp ketchup

3 tbsp tomato paste

1 tsp salt

½ tsp ground white pepper

1 tsp Mediterranean Spice Mix*

¼ tsp of ground ginger

2 large cloves garlic, crushed

¾ cup lemon juice

½ cup olive oil

Combine all ingredients above. If possible, marinate a minimum of one hour (overnight is best!), stirring mixture and chicken several times.

Place in a glass baking dish and bake at 400 degrees for 20 minutes. Move oven rack up high and broil on highest temperature an additional 5 minutes, or until cooked through, browning the top.

Would be great on the grill too!

Lentils & Rice

1 large onion, thinly sliced, lengthwise

3 tbsp olive oil

4 cups chicken broth (I prefer low sodium)

1 cup dried lentils, rinsed

1 cup white or brown rice, uncooked

1 tsp Mediterranean Spice Mix*

Salt and pepper (to taste)

Heat oil in large skillet over High heat. Sauté onions, stirring constantly and continue to cook until slightly browned. Remove ½ of the onions, continue to sauté remaining onions until almost burnt, then remove from skillet and set aside in a separate dish. Return slightly browned onion to skillet. Add remaining ingredients, except for burnt onions, and bring to a boil. Cover and simmer on Low heat for 30–40 minutes, or until all water is absorbed and lentils and rice are soft. Adjust salt and pepper to taste.

Transfer to flat serving plate and flatten lentils and rice in dish. Top with remaining browned onions. Serve warm, cold or at room temperature with pita bread.

*Mediterranean Spice Mix:

- 1 tbsp allspice
- ½ tsp cinnamon
- ½ tsp nutmeg
- ¼ tsp turmeric
- ¼ tsp ground cloves

Keep on hand in an airtight container. Use this spice mix to add a Mediterranean flare to any chicken, vegetable or beef dish.

Blackened Tuscan Swordfish

Ideas for Grilling:

Marinate your swordfish steaks for 1 hour minimum in all listed ingredients, except for the flour. Grill for 2–3 minutes on each side or until middle is white and retains its juice. Avoid over cooking as the fish will become dry and rubbery.

Serve with Minty Potato Salad or Half-the-Time Baked Potatoes, found on pages 72 and 78.

1 lb fresh swordfish

2 tbsp olive oil

1 large clove garlic, minced

½ cup fish stock, clam juice or white wine

Juice of two lemons (or ¼ cup bottled lemon juice)

1 additional lemon, sliced in half—one half cut into wheel shapes for sauté pan, one half cut into small wedges for garnish

¼ tsp dried dill weed

1 tbsp fresh flat leaf parsley, chopped

2 tbsp flour

4 tbsp pitted calamata olives (or 2 tbsp capers, well rinsed)

Freshly ground pepper (to taste)

Rinse fish well and pat dry with paper towel. Lightly flour fish with a mixture of flour, dill weed and ground pepper. Heat olive oil in large skillet on Medium-High heat. Sear each side of swordfish steaks for about 1 minute on each side, turning only once. Squeeze fresh lemon juice and white wine (or fish/clam juice) on top and let simmer uncovered for about 1 minute. Add parsley and calamata olives or capers and sliced lemon wheels to the pan. Cover and cook until swordfish is just cooked through. Be careful not to overcook! Adjust seasonings, adding more lemon juice or stock as necessary. Serve with baked potato or rice pilaf and a quick vegetable side dish (see pages 75–83).

Marinated Salmon Steaks

1 lb fresh or previously frozen salmon steaks

½ cup fresh or bottled lemon juice

1 tbsp stone ground mustard

2 tbsp plain whole or low fat yogurt (do not use fat free)

½ tsp dried dill

White pepper (black pepper is fine too!)

1 whole lemon, cut in wedges

Combine ¼ cup of lemon juice, mustard, yogurt, dill and pepper in a small bowl and mix well.

Place salmon in glass baking dish. Squeeze one or two lemon wedges over salmon and top with marinade. If you have the time, cover and refrigerate for at least one hour to fully absorb the marinade. Otherwise, bake in the oven at 350 degrees for 20–30 minutes, or until cooked through.

Serve with Spanish or Mediterranean rice (pages 75 and 76) and 5-minute Broccoli (page 79).

Marinated Chicken Breasts

1 lb boneless breast of chicken (or breasts with bone)

2 lemons, washed thoroughly (after removing juice, cut rinds into small wedges)

½ cup lemon juice (use juice from 2 fresh lemons and supplement with bottled lemon juice)

¼ cup olive oil

3 large cloves of garlic, minced

¼ tsp cumin

2 tbsp stone ground mustard

6 tbsp plain whole or low fat yogurt (do not use fat free)

Pinch of red pepper flakes

½ tsp hot sauce

Fresh ground black pepper (to taste)

Continues

*Bake at 350 degrees for 45 minutes or until cooked through.

Mix all marinade ingredients together in a large mixing bowl. Place rinsed, trimmed chicken in bowl. Mix well, cover and refrigerate overnight. Grill, broil or bake.*

Pasta Primavera

This is another quick one. Your meal will be done by the time it takes to boil and cook pasta.

1 1-lb box of pasta of your choice

1 10 oz pkg frozen spring vegetables (or any vegetable combination such as carrots, pearl onions, ginger snap peas and green beans)

¼ cup olive oil

1 large clove garlic, minced

¼ tsp sea salt

Freshly ground pepper (to taste)

1 tbsp fresh flat leaf Italian parsley, chopped (or 1 tsp dried)

1 tbsp fresh oregano leaves, chopped (or 1 tsp dried)

1 tbsp fresh basil, chopped (or 1 tsp dried)

Pinch of dried crushed red pepper flakes

½ cup fresh parmasean cheese

Place a large pot of water and bring to boil. Cook pasta according to directions. While pasta is cooking, prepare the sauce by taking a large microwavable bowl with lid and add olive oil, garlic, salt, pepper, crushed red pepper flakes and fresh herbs. Cover with lid and microwave on high for 1 minute, being careful not to burn the garlic. Add frozen vegetables, close lid and microwave on high for 5 minutes. Stir mixture, adjust seasonings and cook a bit more if necessary.

Once pasta is cooked, drain slightly and add vegetables and all of its juice. Mix well, add parmasean cheese and mix again, adjusting seasonings if necessary. Top with add'l grated cheese and fresh herbs. Serve hot or at room temperature.

Add cooked shrimp or diced, cooked chicken to this recipe for a complete meal!

There are some recipes that take a bit more time than this book's 30 minute goal. However, I could not ignore a few because they were a big part of our family culture and some of my favorite meals. The following recipes are for when you have some extra time on your hands and you'd like to prepare one of those "special occasion" family meals.

Grape Leaves

This is one of my all time favorite Lebanese dishes! It took me years to find out how to make grape leaves. My father never knew because he didn't like the idea of having to roll them, so he didn't eat them until someone made them for him. I did the same for years, until I met my good friend Carla. I met her on the football field and we chatted a bit about our families. I found out that she was half Lebanese and we were instantly close friends. Carla makes grape leaves for her family of five all of the time. She gave me the basics on how to prepare these quickly. I've further modified the recipe to lower the fat and add other flavors (see next page for optional additions).

My family likes to eat these hot, warmed, and sometimes room temperature on top of Simple Salad (see page 11).

1 10oz jar pickled grape leaves

2 tbsp olive oil

1 lb ground beef (use extra lean if you are fat conscious, but 80% lean gives this dish more flavor)

¼ tsp each salt, pepper, allspice (or to taste)

The juice of ½ lemon (or ⅛ cup bottled lemon juice)

½ cup white rice, uncooked

2 tbsp water (keep on hand as needed)

Remove half of the grape leaves from jar and rinse well to remove the salt from its pickling juice. The fastest way to do this is to place them in a pot of cold water. Pull the leaves gently apart and gather each by its stem, grabbing about 5 or 6 at a time. Trim the stems using kitchen shears.

Continues

Return the leaves to the pot, shake them into the water, and then transfer to a colander to allow the excess water to drip.

Ideas for your picky eater:

If your kids will not eat grape leaves, before adding the rice to the stuffing mixture, make hamburger patties with the rest of the ingredients and broil or grill while the grape leaves are boiling. Serve with ketchup, with or without a hamburger roll.

Combine rice, ground beef, olive oil, lemon juice, spices and optional ingredients if you choose to use them (see below). Mix well with hands and keep adding water or tomato juice to maintain a moist texture. Place approximately 1 tbsp of mixture in bottom center of one grape leaf.

Roll grape leaf from bottom and fold left and right sides with each roll upward, creating a firm, but not too tight form. Keep in mind that when the rice cooks it will expand, so you'll need to leave room in order to avoid ripped leaves when cooked.

Line grape leaves in a medium saucepan, forming one tight layer at a time. You should have two or three layers, depending on the size of your pan. Pour just enough water in the pan to cover grape leaves. Cover with a tight lid and bring to a boil. Simmer for 30 minutes, or until rice and beef are cooked and leaves are tender to chew.

If you have the time, add the following ingredients to the grape leaves mixture:

- **$1/4$ cup minced onion**
- **one small can petite diced tomatoes AND $1/4$ cup of its juice instead of the water listed on the previous page**
- **one dash crushed red pepper or splash of hot sauce for a spicy flavor**

Serve with plain yogurt, or Tangy Yogurt Spread (see **Lebni** on page 23) on the side.

Uncle Rudy's Pasta Bolognese

Every so often, I'll enjoy an excellent bolognese dish at a fine Italian restaurant, yet none of them compare to my Uncle Rudy's own homemade batch. You can cut out some of the wait time to serve this meal by preparing the sautéing items the night before and placing them all in the crock pot.

1 lb box tagliatelle or ziti pasta

3 tbsp olive oil

1 thick slice of pancetta bacon (about $\frac{1}{8}$ inch thick)

2 carrots (medium sized)

2 stalks celery with leaves

1 large, yellow, Spanish or white onion

2 or 3 cloves of garlic (to taste)

1 cup diced white button or crimini mushrooms

1 lb of lean ground beef

1 lb of ground veal

1 cup of dry red wine

1 cup whole milk

4 oz tomato paste

1 28 oz can crushed tomatoes

Sea salt and pepper (to taste)

1 pinch of red pepper flakes (optional)

1 tbsp fresh parsley, chopped (1 tsp dried parsley)

$\frac{1}{4}$ tsp each dried basil and oregano

$\frac{1}{8}$ tsp thyme

Coarsely chop the pancetta, carrots, celery, onion, and garlic, then place in food processor and grind until they are a bit chunky. Avoid a pasty consistency. Pour 3 tbsp olive oil in large frying pan and set on Medium-High

Continues

heat. Add the vegetables from the food processor. Cook 10 to 15 minutes, or until thickened. Add the ground beef & veal. Mix well and brown for an additional 10–15 minutes. Add tomato paste and cook for another 5 minutes. Add wine. Mix and cook for 5 minutes. Add crushed tomatoes and milk, then stir well. Reduce heat to a low simmer. Add all herbs and seasonings and mix well again. Cover and simmer for approx 2 hours.*

Cook pasta according to your personal taste. *lightly* drain pasta, reserving about ¼ cup of liquid. Return to pot and place over Low heat. Add a few ladles of Bolognese sauce. Mix well.

Serve in large pasta bowls. Line the bowl with the pasta and top with Bolognese sauce. Serve with fresh grated cheese.

* Would be a great time to put it in your crock pot! Follow the recipe up until it's ready for the oven. Place all ingredients in your crock pot. Let cook on High for four hours or on Low for 6–8 hours.

Flavorful Meatballs

For years no one knew what my Aunt Lee put in her meatballs to make them so tasty. She kept her secret ingredient to herself, until she decided to share it with me. Now, you too can enjoy Aunt Lee's Flavorful Meatballs. I have substituted the ground beef with ground turkey for a lower fat option for my family, but you can certainly use ground beef!

1 lb ground turkey or 1 lb ground beef

1 egg, beaten

¼ cup yellow or Vidalia onion, minced

2 tbsp fresh flat leaf parsley, chopped (or 1 tsp dried parsley flakes)

1 tsp dried basil

2 pinches ground cumin

1 cup Italian flavored bread crumbs

2 slices white (or wheat) bread, ends trimmed and bread broken up into bite sized pieces (see footnote below*)

¼ cup fresh grated parmesan cheese

Sea salt and fresh ground pepper (to taste)

Sauce:

4 quarts Aunt Lee's Marinara or your favorite jarred or homemade tomato sauce

2–3 tbsp olive oil (to coat baking dish)

> **Meatballs make great leftovers for lunch or dinner the next day.**
>
> **–OR–**
>
> **Freeze your meatballs!**
>
> **Cook thoroughly in the oven being sure to bake them at 350 degrees.**
>
> **Once fully baked, set aside and cool completely. Place in large freezer bags and freeze until you are ready to serve them.**
>
> **It's convenient to be able to throw a few of the frozen meatballs in a pot of cooked tomato sauce for a quick and healthy meal in a pinch.**

Place tomato sauce in large pot and bring to a simmer.

Place rest of ingredients, except the olive oil, in large mixing bowl. Knead and mend the mixture with your hand until well blended.

In a shallow baking dish or cookie sheet with a small edge, cover entire bottom of pan with about 2–3 tbsp olive oil to ensure a light coating all around. Using either your hands or a medium sized melon or ice cream scoop, form equal sized tight, round balls with the meatball mixture and place about ½ inch apart on oiled baking dish.

Broil in oven on highest broiling temperature and watch carefully for meatballs to brown well on all sides, turning every minute or two. Once meatballs appear crispy all around, use a slotted spoon to carefully drain any extra pan drippings and slowly transfer the meatballs to the pot of sauce. Let simmer on stove until meatballs are cooked through (about 10–15 minutes).

Serve as a main dish. Pour over cooked pasta or make meatball subs.

* If using ground beef instead of turkey, be sure to soak the two pieces of bread in a bowl of water before breaking into pieces. Slightly ring out excess water before adding to the meatball mixture. This liquid is necessary to add in order to avoid a dry meatball. Ground turkey is naturally more moist and doesn't require the water.

There's nothing better than being with good friends and family on a beautiful summer day with a light summer menu to look forward to. I brought the drink mentioned below to a neighbor's pool one evening and I shared it with everyone. They loved it so much, one of my neighbors named it, "Lisa's Lazy Summer Lemonade". This is a great drink for family and friends. In the pages that follow you will get other quick and fresh ideas that I have enjoyed with my family and friends each summer.

Lisa's Lazy Summer Lemonade

¾ cup granulated sugar

¾ cup bottled lemon juice

1 tbsp fresh orange rind

1 whole orange, sliced in half pinwheel shapes

5 or 6 mint leaves, torn or chopped into large pieces

½ gallon drinking water with about 4 cups ice

In a small saucepan, combine 2 cups of water with sugar, and cook on Medium-Low heat until sugar dissolves. Pour melted sugar & water in a large pitcher filled with ice. Add rest of the ingredients and mix well. Store in refrigerator until ready to serve. When serving, pour into individual glasses filled with ice, being sure to sift out the orange and mint leaves. Top with a fresh mint leaf.

Other ideas for your summer drink:

This drink makes for a great mixer to be used with your favorite alcohol.

Iced Mint Tea

This recipe uses all ingredients listed in Lisa's Lazy Summer Lemonade, but I've substituted the cold drinking water and ½ gallon of boiled water with 5 tea bags (decaf or regular).

¾ cup granulated sugar

¾ cup bottled lemon juice

1 tbsp fresh orange rind

1 whole orange, sliced in half pinwheel shape

5 or 6 mint leaves, torn or chopped into large pieces

½ gallon boiled water with about 5 tea bags (decaf or regular)

4 cups ice

Combine the ingredients and add ice immediately*.

*If you'd like a less sweet variation, try adding more water to the mix. More lemon juice and/or orange slices will also change the taste to your liking.

Quick Gazpacho

This cold Spanish soup has been a favorite of mine for many years. I have tasted several variations of it, but I prefer it blended in a food processor or blender rather than chopped. Fresh herbs make this first course a big hit with friends. This is my quick version. No need to seed, core and peel tomatoes— unless, of course you have the time.

¼ cup loosely packed fresh cilantro and flat leaf parsley
    leaves with some of the stems

4 leaves fresh oregano (or ½ tsp dried)

¼ tsp ground cumin

1 dash of red pepper flakes (optional)

Sea salt (to taste)

2 tsp fresh lemon juice (or 1 tbsp bottled)

2 whole ice cubes

1 15.5 oz can stewed tomatoes with juice

1 large, firm English cucumber, peeled and diced into large chunks

½ red, yellow or orange pepper, diced

1 celery stick, coarsely chopped

1 small clove garlic

2 tbsp *mild* onion (like yellow or scallion), diced, including some
    of the greens

Sour cream for topping

Keep it simple:

If you don't have all of the ingredients handy, you can use just the canned tomatoes, cucumber, garlic and herbs.

Experiment with your favorite vegetables!

Place all ingredients in a blender or food processor (except sour cream) and puree for approximately 1 minute. Check for smooth, but grainy consistency. Garnish with fresh chopped cilantro and sour cream and serve.

Store leftovers in airtight container in refrigerator. Will keep for a few days.

For leftovers:

You can use the remaining Gazpacho soup as a base for a tasty meat chili.

Just heat in a crock pot or stockpot and add cooked ground beef or turkey and a can of red kidney beans.

Uncle John's Grilled Lemon & Garlic Chicken

**Mediterranean Spice Mix:

- 1 tbsp allspice
- ½ tsp cinnamon
- ½ tsp nutmeg
- ¼ tsp turmeric
- ¼ tsp ground cloves

Keep on hand in an airtight container. Use this spice mix to add a Mediterranean flare to any chicken, vegetable or beef dish.

I have very fond memories of my childhood; enjoying my uncle's grilled dishes during the summer months. He would marinate a whole cut up chicken for several days, creating a robust flavor that was very difficult to duplicate. But now, I've learned his secret.

1 whole bone-in chicken, cut into parts

4 large cloves fresh garlic, minced (or 6 small cloves)

¼ cup olive oil

1 large white onion quartered

¼ cup dry white wine

3 whole *very ripe* lemons, hand squeezed with ½ of the rinds cut into wedges

Add'l fresh or bottled lemon juice (if needed)

2 tbsp stone ground mustard*

1 tbsp tomato paste

½ cup loosely packed fresh, chopped flat leaf parsley

¼ cup mint, chopped

1 tsp sea salt (or to taste)

Black pepper (or to taste)

2 tsp Mediterranean Spice Mix**

Dash of hot sauce (optional)

Combine all ingredients, including the lemon rinds. Taste marinade, adding add'l lemon juice, as necessary to suit your taste. Reserve ¼ cup of marinade for basting. Pour the rest over uncooked chicken in an air tight container. Marinate in refrigerator overnight. Grill chicken pieces on High flame, searing the outside of the meat and basting occasionally with marinade. Slow cook on Low flame until chicken runs clear with juice when pierced.

* Try horseradish mustard for a spicy option.

Grilled Marinated Swordfish

You may choose to use tuna steaks instead. Both thick and meaty fish choices are great on the grill.

2 tbsp olive oil

1 large clove garlic, minced

½ cup fish stock (can also use clam juice or white wine)

½ cup lemon juice

1 lemon, sliced in half with one half cut into wheel shape for sauté pan, the other half cut in small wedges for garnish

½ tsp dried dill

2 tbsp flat leaf parsley, chopped

1 lb fresh swordfish or tuna steaks

Freshly ground pepper (to taste)

Rinse fish well and pat dry with paper towel. Marinate fish with all listed Ingredients for a minimum of one hour, turning fish over every so often to ensure that marinade soaks evenly.

Heat grill on High temperature. Once hot, sear the swordfish, grilling for one minute on each side. Flip again and continue to brush marinade on fish often. Cook for additional 3–5 minutes on each side, to taste. If using swordfish, be sure that the middle just turns white and remains juicy, not too dry. Serve with extra lemon wedges.

Serve your fish with:

Mediterranean Rice and Mediterranean grilled vegetables. See pages 73 and 75 for details.

*Mediterranean Spice Mix:

- **1 tbsp allspice**
- **½ tsp cinnamon**
- **½ tsp nutmeg**
- **¼ tsp turmeric**
- **¼ tsp ground cloves**

Keep on hand in an airtight container. Use this spice mix to add a Mediterranean flare to any chicken, vegetable or beef dish.

Shish Kebab

1 lb lamb meat or sirloin, cubed and tenderized with a mallet. (cut about 3 inches thick)

2 large cloves garlic, minced

1 small onion, minced

⅓ cup olive oil

½ cup fresh flat leaf Italian parsley, finely chopped

¼ cup fresh mint, finely chopped

1 tsp salt

1 tsp Mediterranean Spice Mix*

Fresh ground black pepper to taste

Approx 20 large cherry tomatoes or 3 large, firm red tomatoes, quartered then cut in half

1 small pkg whole white mushroom, brushed clean

3 add'l large onions, peeled and quartered

Combine oil, garlic, minced onion and spices in a large bowl. Stir in meat and coat well. Marinate in refrigerator for at least one hour (overnight is best!). Be sure to stir the mixture up a few times, ensuring a full marinade on all sides.

Using either stainless steel or bamboo skewers*, thread meat, onion, tomatoes and mushrooms onto skewers, alternating the ingredients.

Grill over hot flame, turning several times until tender and browned (*about 8 minutes*).

Serve hot with pita bread.

Serve with Sito's Fatoosh (on page 18) and Minty Potato Salad (on page 72).

* If you use bamboo skewers, soak in water and 1 tsp oil for about ½ hour before using to keep the exposed portions from burning.

Marinated Steak Tips

1–1 ½ lb steak tips, tenderized with a mallet

¼ cup olive oil

3 cloves garlic, minced

½ cup red wine vinegar

¼ cup dry red wine

½ cup low sodium soy sauce

1 large red onion, quartered (keep pieces large for grilling)

1 tsp dried oregano (or 1 tbsp fresh)

1 tsp basil (or 3 fresh leaves)

½ tsp fresh ground black pepper

Place all marinade ingredients in a large bowl with an airtight lid. Mix well, and then combine steak with marinade, making sure that the steak is well drenched and covered completely. Cover tightly and place in refrigerator for at least one hour— over night is ideal!

Grill steak on High flame, searing on both sides. Lower flame and cook 3 – 5 minutes on each side, depending on the thickness of the steak and desired doneness.

Minty Potato Salad

1 bag small Red Bliss potatoes

1 small red onion, diced into small cubes

¼ cup extra virgin olive oil

¼–⅓ cup *chilled* fresh lemon juice, or bottled (or to taste)

¼ cup loosely packed fresh mint, finely chopped

1 small clove garlic, minced

Sea salt and pepper (to taste)

Scrub dirt off of potatoes and place in large pot of cold water.

Bring water to boil, then simmer potatoes for 10 minutes, or until potatoes are firm, but not too hard when pierced with a fork. Drain potatoes and immediately place in mixing bowl. Drizzle with ¼ cup of the chilled lemon juice, reserving the rest if needed, and remaining ingredients. Toss gently. Adjust seasonings, adding more lemon juice, salt and pepper as needed. Refrigerate for at least one hour and serve cold.

Mediterranean Grilled Vegetables

To make this quick favorite, put whatever fresh or frozen vegetables you have on hand in a large tin foil bag, add olive oil and seasonings and cook on a Low flame, or on the highest rack on your grill. The veggies will steam while your meats are grilling.

2 small zucchinis, sliced lengthwise, about 3 inches long

1 cup match stick sized carrots

½ small Vidalia or other sweet onion, sliced thin and lengthwise

3 tbsp pitted calamata olives

Small handful of combined fresh parsley and mint, coarsely chopped

2 tbsp olive oil

Salt and pepper (to taste)

Place all vegetables in a dish lined with tin foil. In a small mixing bowl, combine olive oil, calamata olives, salt, pepper and herbs. Pour mixture over vegetables. Fold tin foil at the top and sides to prevent leaking. Grill on Low heat, or on highest rack, and allow to steam as your grilled meats are cooking.

In order to save time and make less trips to the grocery store, I have learned to buy my vegetables frozen and in bulk. As for non perishable items, keeping brown and white rice in the pantry is always handy if you need a starch to serve with your meal. But plain rice can be boring, so in the pages that follow, I have listed some ideas to add variety to a basic rice dish.

Mediterranean Rice

2 tbsp olive oil

2 tbsp white or yellow onion, or scallions including a bit of the green, diced

1 small clove garlic, minced

½ tsp sea salt (or to taste)

¼ tsp Mediterranean Spice Mix*

1 cup basmati brown rice, uncooked

1 10 oz can chickpeas, well drained

2 cups low sodium chicken broth

In a large microwavable dish with lid, combine olive oil, onion, garlic and salt and mix well. Place uncovered in microwave and cook on High for 2 minutes. Add remaining ingredients. Cover and cook again on High for 5 minutes, then cook another 20 minutes at 50% power until all of the water is absorbed. Gently mix rice with fork and serve hot.

*Mediterranean Spice Mix:

- 1 tbsp allspice
- ½ tsp cinnamon
- ½ tsp nutmeg
- ¼ tsp turmeric
- ¼ tsp ground cloves

Keep on hand in an airtight container. Use this spice mix to add a Mediterranean flare to any chicken, vegetable or beef dish.

Spanish Rice

This recipe is similar to the Mediterranean rice and it is quickly done in the microwave, allowing you to cook your main meal and not have to check on the rice until it's time to serve.

2 tbsp olive oil

½ white or green onion, finely chopped

1 cup white or brown rice, uncooked

1 tsp cilantro base

1 tsp lime juice

2 or 3 sprigs fresh cilantro, chopped (or 1/4 tsp ground coriander)

2 cups water

Sea salt and pepper (to taste)

Place olive oil and onions in a microwavable dish. Microwave uncovered on High heat for 30 seconds. Stir and cook 20–30 seconds more until onions are translucent, but not browned. Add the remaining ingredients and follow microwave cooking instructions for your rice.

Indian Rice

This rice dish takes a bit more time, but it's well worth it. Serve with an Indian main course such as Tandoori Chicken, found on page 43.

1 cup basmati or wild rice blend (combination of white, brown, wild & red rice)

2 tbsp olive oil

¼ cup slivered almonds

1 small onion, diced

1 large clove of garlic, minced

2 tsp Indian Spice Mix*

2 cups chicken broth, heated

Heat oil in a medium sized pot over Medium heat until hot. Cook almonds, stirring frequently until golden brown. Transfer with slotted spoon to paper towels to drain, then add onion to pot and cook over Medium High heat, stirring frequently, until pale golden. Add garlic and Indian Spice Mix. Continue to stir for about 6 more minutes. Add broth and bring to a simmer. Cover and continue to cook an additional 15 minutes, or until all liquid is absorbed. Remove from heat and let stand covered for an additional 5 minutes. Uncover and fluff with fork. Top with slivered almonds and serve immediately.

* Indian Spice Mix:
Keep on hand in an air tight container a combination of the following spices:

- 1 tbsp ground cumin
- 1 tsp ground coriander
- ½ tsp cayenne pepper
- ½ tsp dried ground ginger
- ¼ tsp ground cloves
- ¼ tsp fresh ground black pepper
- 1 tsp salt

Half-the-Time Fresh Baked Potatoes

*Mediterranean Spice Mix:

- **1 tbsp allspice**
- **½ tsp cinnamon**
- **½ tsp nutmeg**
- **¼ tsp turmeric**
- **¼ tsp ground cloves**

Keep on hand in an airtight container. Use this spice mix to add a Mediterranean flare to any chicken, vegetable or beef dish.

4 large Idaho Potatoes, washed and scrubbed

Olive oil

Sea salt

½ tsp Allspice (or Mediterranean Spice Mix*)

Preheat oven to 450 degrees. Cut each potato in half, lengthwise. With a fork pierce the top part of the potato and drag the fork all the way down, creating lengthwise piercing. Prick holes with the fork randomly around the potato pulp. Drizzle ½ tsp olive oil on each potato half and sprinkle with sea salt and a pinch of spices. Place in Microwave pulp side up and cook on High for 5 minutes. Place potato halves on oven rack (pulp side up) in oven at 450 degrees for about 20 minutes, or until center is soft when pierced with a fork.

Candied Sweet Potatoes

4 large whole sweet potatoes, peeled

1 tsp cinnamon

1 tsp nutmeg

1 tsp sugar

Aside from cucumbers, this sweet treat side dish is the only vegetable my son will eat!

Preheat oven to 450 degrees. Place whole sweet potatoes in microwave for 5 minutes. Carefully place potatoes in oven, and bake 20–25 minutes, or until soft when pierced with a fork. While potatoes are cooking, combine the cinnamon, nutmeg and sugar.

Remove from oven and let cool slightly. Cut each potato in half lengthwise and sprinkle with sweet spices. Serve hot.

5-Minute Lemon Broccoli

2 cups frozen broccoli florettes

2 tbsp olive oil

2 tbsp lemon juice (or to taste)

Sea salt (to taste)

Place all ingredients in microwavable dish with lid and mix well. Cook on High for 3½ minutes. Stir and check tenderness. For a softer broccoli, cook an additional 1–2 minutes..

5-Minute Cooked Spinach

2 cups frozen chopped spinach

2 tbsp olive oil

Sea salt (to taste)

½ small clove garlic, minced or dash of garlic powder (optional)

Place all ingredients in microwavable dish with lid and mix well. Cook on High for 3 minutes. Stir and check to see if spinach is cooked through and is hot. If spinach is still frozen or is not hot, cook an additional 1–2 minutes.

5-minute Bean Medley

Use any combination of beans that you have handy, creating a nice combination that your family will enjoy. I have suggested a four-bean medley that's a favorite in my household.

2 cups frozen combination green, yellow and wax beans

½ of a 15.5 oz can garbanzo beans with 2 tbsp of its juice

½ small onion, diced

2 tbsp fresh lemon juice (or bottled)

1 dash garlic powder

1 tsp dried basil

2 tbsp olive oil

¼ tsp sea salt (or to taste)

Mix all ingredients well. Place in microwavable dish with a lid. Cook covered on High heat for 3 minutes. Stir well and cook an additional 2 minutes, or until beans are cooked to your liking.

Sautéed Green Beans with Tomatoes and Garlic

(Luby)

2 lbs fresh green beans, ends trimmed or (frozen green beans, full length)

1 28 oz can of stewed tomatoes, sliced and drained

1 large onion, chopped

2 cloves garlic, crushed

3 tbsp olive oil

1 tbsp lemon juice

Salt and pepper (to taste)

2 tsp Mediterranean Spice Mix*

Pinch of crushed red pepper flakes (optional, or to taste)

*Mediterranean Spice Mix:

- 1 tbsp allspice
- ½ tsp cinnamon
- ½ tsp nutmeg
- ¼ tsp turmeric
- ¼ tsp ground cloves

Keep on hand in an airtight container. Use this spice mix to add a Mediterranean flare to any chicken, vegetable or beef dish.

Heat oil in a saucepan. Add onions and sauté until soft. Add garlic and beans. Cook on Low heat for 15 minutes, or until the beans start to wilt. Add the tomatoes, lemon juice, salt and pepper. Cover and cook on Low heat for an additional 15 minutes. Cook longer for a softer green bean.

Serve cold or warm with pita bread.

Sautéed Chickpeas

I think chickpeas are one of the most underrated foods. They're packed with protein, low in fat, and can be added to almost any dish—salads, stews, and side dishes—served hot or cold. This is a fast way to get a healthy, low-fat protein dish to complement any main course.

1 15.5 oz can chickpeas, drained

2 tbsp olive oil

2 cloves garlic, minced

$\frac{1}{8}$ cup fresh lemon juice (or bottled)

Heat oil over Medium heat. Sauté garlic and chickpeas. Once chickpeas appear soft, add lemon juice. Cook for approximately 10 minutes.

Ratatouille

1 large clove garlic, minced

3 tbsp olive oil

1 medium Vidalia onion, diced

1 12 oz can diced stewed tomatoes, drained

1 medium sized zucchini, sliced into ¼ inch rounds

1 small summer squash, sliced into ¼ inch rounds

1 small eggplant, peeled and cubed

2 tbsp fresh flat leaf parsley, chopped (or 1 tsp dried)

1 tbsp fresh basil, chopped (or 1 tsp dried)

1 tsp dried oregano

Sea salt and ground black pepper (to taste)

Heat oil in large skillet. Add onion and herbs and sauté until onions are translucent (about 2 minutes). Add garlic and cook for about 30 seconds, then add remaining ingredients. Bring to a simmer and cover. Cook for 15 minutes, or until vegetables are slightly tender and flavors have blended in well. Adjust seasonings as necessary.

I have learned over the years to stay away from desserts in general. They are usually filled with butter, lard and white flour—none of which are very good for you. It's nice to have a few dessert recipes on hand that are on the lower-fat end, and healthy enough so that no guilt is involved when you need to indulge every once in a while! My husband and kids love these lower-fat, low-cholesterol treats.

Lower-fat Baklava

2 cups pistachio nuts, chopped

⅓ cup sugar

1 tsp rose water (found in Ethnic markets, but can be found in the International isle of some large supermarkets)

1 lb filo dough

1 lb non-hydrogenated margarine (or 50/50 margarine/butter blend)

Syrup recipe:

- 2 cups sugar
- 1 cup water
- few drops of lemon juice
- 1 tsp rose water

Continues

In a medium-sized bowl, combine nuts, sugar and rose water. Spread filo dough in a buttered 10x14 inch pan, brushing each layer with the butter/margarine blend. Half way through the layering, place nut mixture in ½ to ¾ inch layer.

Continue layering buttered filo on top. Cut into diamond shaped pieces. Bake at 300 degrees for one hour, or until golden brown.

While baking, place all syrup ingredients in small pot and bring to a boil.

Once baklava is cooked, pour syrup over pastry, making sure that the dough is well saturated.

Serve at room temperature.

Greek Shortbread Cookies

(Kourambiedes)

As a child I can remember moving into a new neighborhood and meeting a nice Greek family. The mother would make these Kourambiedes for us on special occasions. I loved them so much that each time I saw her I would ask her when she was planning on making them again. I could never pronounce the name, so I would call them "Cookie Eddies". Well, I hadn't had a "Cookie Eddie" like that for over 20 years until one day, our company's office manager brought them to work the day after Greek Easter. I was in heaven! She never forgot to save me a few after each Greek holiday. She would even hide some for me so the other employees couldn't eat them all before I got into work.

I have asked her on occasion to get the exact recipe for me, but she couldn't pry it out of her aunt. A secret recipe it was indeed! As a compromise, Sandy found a recipe for me in one of her traditional Greek cookbooks. Now that I cut out a bit of the guilt, substituting some of the white flour with whole wheat and cutting out half the fat, I can enjoy these even more. Her aunt would be mortified knowing that I tampered with perfection!

1 cup 50/50 non-hydrogenated margarine & butter softened

½ cup confectioner's sugar

1 egg yoke (or egg yolk substitute)

1 tbsp + ⅛ tsp ouzo or brandy

1¾ cups whole wheat flour

¾ cup white flour

1 cup ground almonds

1½ cups additional confectioner's sugar for dredging

Continues

Put the softened butter and confectioner's sugar in a large bowl and beat until pale and fluffy. Beat in the egg and ouzo (or brandy). Gradually add the flour and almonds to form a soft, firm dough. Using your hands, mend the mixture thoroughly creating a moist texture.

Cut the dough into 24 pieces and knead well. Roll into firm round balls, about ½ inch in diameter. Press down slightly on an ungreased cookie sheet to flatten the bottom. Place each cookie far apart enough to allow room for them to spread slightly.

Bake in a 350 degree oven for 18–20 minutes, or until firm to the touch and light golden brown. While the cookies are baking, sift a layer of confectioner's sugar into a large flat serving dish or unused cookie sheet.

Once baked, allow the cookies to cool slightly, then place on the prepared dish or cookie sheet in a single layer, and roll the cookies around the sugar. Place the cookies neatly around a plate, sift additional confectioner's sugar generously on top, and let cool for a few hours. Store cookies in an airtight tin with any remaining confectioner's sugar, so that they remain coated.

Rice Pudding

1 cup white rice

3 cups whole milk (for a lighter version, use no less than 2% milk)

2 cups water

1 cup granulated sugar

1 tbsp rose water

½ cup slivered almonds

In a large saucepan, cook rice in water for 15 minutes. Add milk and stir until the mixture becomes thick. Add rose water and sugar. Continue stirring until rice is done. Place in individual serving bowls and chill in refrigerator.

Sprinkle with slivered almonds before serving.

Italian (Anise) Cookies

½ cup 50/50 blend of non-hydrogenated margarine & butter, softened

½ cup white sugar

1 whole egg

2 egg whites

1 tsp vanilla extract

1¼ tsp anise extract or Anisette liquor

1¾ cups all-purpose white flour

1 cup whole wheat flour

2 tsp baking powder

Vegetable oil spray

Glaze:

½ cup confectioner's sugar

1–2 tbsp water

Colored sugar sprinkles (multi color)

Preheat oven to 350 degrees. Lightly spray cookie sheets with vegetable oil.

In a large bowl, cream together the butter and sugar until smooth. Mix in the egg, vanilla, and anise. Combine the flour and baking powder and stir into the creamed mixture until blended. Divide dough into walnut sized portions and roll each piece into a 3 inch ball. Flatten the bottom of each cookie by pressing down on the top as you place them on the cookie sheet 2 inches apart. Bake for 8 to 10 minutes until firm and golden around the edges.

While the cookies are cooling, prepare glaze. Place confectioner's sugar in a small pan over low heat. Add one tbsp water and mix well. Add additional drops of water and stir until desired consistency is reached. Remove from heat and slightly cool. Add 2 tbsp colored sugar and mix well. Take cooled cookies one at a time and dip rounded side in sugar mixture. Return to cookie sheet or serving dish. Keep covered.

Almond Biscotti

(Makes about 3 dozen)

½ cup 50/50 blend of non-hydrogenated margarine & butter, softened

3 eggs (or egg substitute)

¾ cup loosely packed brown sugar

1 tbsp anise or almond extract

1½ cups whole wheat flour

1½ cups all purpose white flour

1 tbsp baking powder

½ tsp salt

1 cup slivered almonds

Preheat oven to 375 degrees. Grease baking sheets.

In a bowl, combine the butter, eggs, sugar, and anise extract. Add the flour, baking powder and almonds. Mix well.

Divide the dough into 2 pieces. Shape each piece into a 1–½ x 14-inch log. Place on prepared baking sheets about 2 inches apart.

Bake about 25 minutes or until lightly browned.

Remove sheet from oven and place on a rack for 10 minutes to cool. **Keep oven heated.**

Transfer logs to a cutting surface. Using a serrated knife, cut the logs diagonally into ½–inch thick slices. Place the slices cut side down onto the baking sheet. Bake 10–12 minutes, or until dry.

Cool on wire racks.

Low-fat, Low-cholesterol Chocolate Chip Cookies

Although chocolate chip cookies are not considered "Mediterranean", given that these are lower in fat, and lower in cholesterol certainly makes them "New American" in my book.

Makes about 40 3-inch round cookies

1 $\frac{1}{4}$ cups whole wheat flour

$\frac{3}{4}$ cup white flour

$\frac{1}{4}$ cup white sugar

$\frac{1}{2}$ cup loosely packed brown sugar

1 whole egg, well beaten

2 egg whites, well beaten

$\frac{1}{2}$ cup 50/50 margarine/butter blend, softened

1 tsp baking powder

$\frac{1}{2}$ tsp salt

1 $\frac{1}{2}$ cups chocolate chip morsels

A pinch each of allspice and cinnamon

$\frac{1}{2}$ tsp vanilla extract

Preheat oven to 350 degrees. In a large mixing bowl mix sugar, brown sugar, butter, vanilla and eggs in a large bowl by hand. Stir in flour, baking soda, and salt and mix well until fully moistened. Stir in chocolate chips and blend well.

Using two teaspoons, scoop about 1 rounded tsp of mixture and place on a non-stick cookie sheet about 2 inches apart. Bake for 12–15 minutes or until brown on the sides. Let cool for a few minutes then place cookies on cooling rack and allow to cool completely.

Low-fat, Low-cholesterol Congo Bars

Another all American dessert, but much healthier.

Makes about 30 3-inch square bars

1½ cups whole wheat flour

1 cup white flour

¾ cup packed brown sugar

1 whole egg, lightly beaten

2 egg whites, lightly beaten

1¼ sticks 50/50 margarine/butter blend, softened

2 tsp baking powder

¼ tsp salt

¼ tsp Allspice

¼ Cinnamon

1½ cups chocolate chip morsels

Preheat oven to 375 degrees. Grease & flour a 10×15 baking dish or brownie pan.

Beat butter and sugar in bowl until creamy. Add eggs and beat well. Stir in flour, baking powder, salt and cinnamon. Blend well until fully moistened. Fold in chips.

Pour mixture into baking dish. Bake for 25–30 minutes, or until brown on the sides and when the center is pierced with a knife or toothpick, it comes out clean.

Let cool completely before cutting into squares.

✳ Planning Ahead ✳

I have always heard how you should plan your meals in advance and go to the grocery store with ideas in mind for the week. But I still have a hard time guessing what my family will be in the mood for, what I will feel like cooking, and quite honestly, figuring out when in the heck I will have the time to fix a meal between the kids' activities, homework, work, house chores, etc.

As a result, I have learned to keep some non-perishable items on hand in the pantry or freezer to help make meal time less of a hassle. I am a big fan of freezing anything that can be frozen. For example, my family goes through bread like crazy. I found myself always having to stop at the store two or three times a week to pick up more, which took up more of my precious time.

Now, I freeze bread. I buy it fresh when it's convenient to go to a wholesale store, or at my local grocery store when the price is just right. I buy five or six loaves at a time and place them right in the freezer when I get home.

Other items that I buy frozen are vegetables. Frozen vegetables are just as good, if not better than fresh vegetables, because they are frozen very shortly after they are picked. Fresh vegetables are usually stored in warehouses for days before they reach you, which, to me, doesn't sound very appealing—or healthy. By purchasing frozen versions instead, I almost never run out of our daily allowance of green leafy vegetables. Broccoli florettes and chopped frozen spinach, for example, can be bought at wholesale clubs in

95

bulk. They usually come packaged with smaller plastic containers inside the large cardboard packaging, so you don't have to separate and bag these items yourself, like you would with meats.

Another good deal that I find at these wholesale clubs is the large quantity of frozen, boneless, skinless, chicken tenderloins that's available for a very reasonable price. These come trimmed, ready to cook, and in one large resealable bag, not stuck together in one clump. When I need a few of them, I simply go into the freezer, take what I need, and I cook with them immediately. I find they thaw out very quickly, so there's no need to defrost beforehand.

Another staple that I always like to have on hand, but is quite perishable, is fresh herbs. A lot of people underestimate the flavor of fresh, flat-leaf Italian parsley. I use this herb in almost *everything*. However, in the past, I found myself buying a variety of fresh herbs for only one recipe and needing only one or two tablespoons of each. I ended up discarding the rest since I had no use for it later in the week, or it would sit in my refrigerator and rot. My solution was to grow my own. I have three small pots that I keep in my house by a sunny window during the fall and winter months. Those herbs are parsley, basil and mint. So when I only need one tablespoon of chopped fresh parsley, I go to my plant and pick what I need. No waste and no extra purchase necessary. Of course, the Italian and Lebanese in me finally started to grow a garden a few years ago. So in the late spring and all through the fall, I have an abundance of fresh herbs and vegetables at my fingertips.

Some of the staples that I would recommend keeping for future use are listed below. You should always keep these items on hand in case you suddenly have a strong desire to cook something satisfying. The rest can be purchased when you know for sure that you will be preparing a particular meal.

Pantry Items:

- 2 large cans (28 oz each) stewed tomatoes
- 1 6.5 oz can tomato paste
- 2 15 oz can diced tomatoes
- 2 6.5 oz cans minced clams
- 1 bottle clam juice
- Dried wild mushrooms (I prefer porcini, but crimini are nice too)
- 1 5 lb bag all purpose potatoes
- 1 small bag yellow onions
- Bottled lemon juice (high quality)
- Olive oil (both regular and extra virgin)
- Sweet balsamic vinegar
- Sea salt
- Crushed red pepper
- Dried basil
- Garlic powder
- Allspice
- 1 16 oz can quartered artichoke hearts
- 2 15.5 oz cans chickpeas
- 1 large can (or two 15.5 oz cans) cannellini, or white kidney beans
- Pasta of your choice: I like to keep two boxes of linguini or angel hair, and a few boxes of elbows and ziti.

Foods that can be Frozen for Future Use:

Ideal when purchased at a wholesale club

- Bread (Italian baguette for those special dinners and everyday bread that the family will use on a daily basis)
- Frozen green, leafy vegetables (broccoli, spinach, etc.)

- Frozen green beans
- Chicken and ground meats (turkey or beef)
- Stewing beef
- Fish (flaky, white fish and frozen shrimp)

Fresh Herbs

I cannot say enough about having some fresh herbs in the house. Small herb plants are inexpensive and will save you both time and money in the long run. Not to mention, having them on hand is very convenient if you truly do appreciate the flavors that fresh herbs add to any meal. I suggest the following:

- Italian flat leaf parsley
- Basil
- Cilantro
- Mint
- Oregano

If maintaining all five herb plants is too much for you to manage, try growing just the parsley and cilantro. Both fresh herbs make quite a difference when used versus the dried versions. I find that dried basil, oregano and mint still maintain a nice flavor if the fresh variations are not handy.

Enjoy!

❋ About the Author ❋

*L*isa Akoury-Ross lives in East Bridgewater, Massachusetts with her husband and two children. A veteran of the book publishing business, serving large companies in the Education, Banking and Trade industries for over 20 years, Mrs. Ross has now branched out on her own to create Sweet Dreams Publishing of Massachusetts.

This fledgling company focuses on individual authors who want to publish their books at an affordable price and enjoy the generous royalties that they deserve.

Lisa Akoury-Ross began Sweet Dreams Publishing during the construction of this book. During that time, she lost a close cousin to ALS, also known as Lou Gehrig's Disease. In honor of her dear friend and family member, Leonard Tomasini, a portion of the royalties of this publication will go to the ALS Foundation in the Greater Bay Area of California.

GO TEAM LEO!

For more information on Sweet Dreams Publishing of Massachusetts, visit us online at www.PublishAtSweetDreams.com

CPSIA information can be obtained
at www.ICGtesting.com
Printed in the USA
LVIC010917240313
325675LV00003B